The End of Utopia

The End of Utopia

A Study of Aldous Huxley's
Brave New World

Peter Edgerly Firchow

Lewisburg
Bucknell University Press
London and Toronto: Associated University Presses

Associated University Presses
440 Forsgate Drive
Cranbury, NJ 08512

Associated University Presses
25 Sicilian Avenue
London WC1A 2QH, England

Associated University Presses
2133 Royal Windsor Drive
Unit 1
Mississauga, Ontario
Canada L5J 1K5

Library of Congress Cataloging in Publication Data

Firchow, Peter Edgerly, 1973–
   The end of Utopia.

   Bibliography: p.
   Includes index.
   Huxley, Aldous, 1894–1965.   Brave new world.
2. Huxley, Aldous, 1894–1965—Political and social views.
3. Utopias in literature.   4. Dystopias in literature.
5. Forecasting in literature.   I. Huxley, Aldous, 1894–
1965.   Brave new world.   II. Title.
PR6015.U9B674   1984   823'.912   82-74490
ISBN 0-8387-5058-3

For Leonard Unger

"Ironic points of light
Flash out wherever the Just
Exchange their messages."

Contents

Preface

This is a book about a book, about *Brave New World*. It is a book that seeks to elucidate *Brave New World* literarily, historically, socially, politically, scientifically. Its operating assumption is that the more knowledge—of all kinds—one brings to a work of literature, the greater and the deeper one's enjoyment of that work of literature, as literature, will be. This is not, however, a book that presumes to say the last word about *Brave New World* or even to take into account all the words that have been said about it. It is emphatically not a summary of criticism about Huxley's novel; it is rather an attempt to point the way for new and different sorts of criticism. As for last words, they cannot be spoken about works of art of the stature of *Brave New World;* or if they can, then only because we have approximated the condition it so vividly describes.

This is also a book about a "new world," about a future that seems more possible and less brave with every passing day. *Brave New World* is one of those books—like *Candide* or *1984*—which are not content to be like other books; it does not merely reflect and embody life, but shapes it. The right response to Huxley's satire is not, or is not only, one of admiration at the brilliance of his literary imagination; it is one of horror at who we are and who, or rather what, we may become. The right response to *Brave New World* is to live our lives so as to prevent the coming of the brave new world; the right response is increased awareness.

The form of Huxley's vision is, as with any great work of literature, unique, though it is inevitably part of a tradition. The substance of his vision Huxley shares with many of the important writers of his time: it is the vision of the end of the world as we know it. For Eliot that world ends in a whimper; for Yeats with the slouchings of a rough beast; for Forster with the roar of the bulldozer; for Frost with universal fire or ice; for Orwell in subjection to Big Brother; for Huxley in the transformation of man into a godlike machine. Modern literature is steeped in eschatology, much like the literature of the Middle Ages, and perhaps for the same reasons; for modern weapons and modern technology— including the technologies of individual and mass control—have made the end of the world once again imaginable.

Before the world ends, however, I would like to take this opportunity to thank those who have been involved, in one way or another, in the evolution of this book: the Graduate School of the University of Minnesota for granting me sabbatical leave; the Sprachatlas of the University of Marburg for a quiet desk and a functioning typewriter; Inga Velde, for help in matters bibliographical; my wife, Evelyn Scherabon Firchow, for much advice and understanding; and my daughter, Pamina, for occasional outbursts of patience. I know of course that I am also indebted to many others who have written on *Brave New World;* on Huxley; or on utopian/dystopian literature in general. Some of that debt is acknowledged in the notes and bibliography; if much remains unacknowledged, it is not because I am ungrateful. It is simply that if one wishes to present one's own point of view as clearly and forcefully as possible, one must either raise one's voice so as to drown out the voices of others, or else not be forced into shouting by limiting the volume and number of those other voices. *Dove si grida,* as Leonardo da Vinci remarked, *non è la vera scienza.* I have therefore chosen the latter course.

Finally, there is a debt to three journals who gave portions of this book an earlier home: *Modern Fiction Studies* 12 (Winter 1966–67): 451–60, in which some parts of the first chapter were originally published; and *Contemporary Literature* 16 (Summer 1975): 301–16, and *Journal of Modern Literature* 5 (April 1976): 200–18, where in somewhat different form the second and third chapters, respectively, first appeared. I am grateful to all three for permission to reprint my work here.

The End of Utopia

1
The Future as Literature

Q.: "What should you most like to do, to know, to be?"
A.: "To know more about human beings and to be a better novelist."

"Aldous Huxley," *The Little Review*

All of Mr. Huxley's books are confessions, first cynically triumphant and then despairing, of his inability to be poet or mystic or ironist enough to achieve this transcendence and find in his animal heritage a satisfaction for his spiritual needs. . . . Exercising the most perverse ingenuity in confronting romance with biology and in establishing the identity (in the realm of fact) of love and lust, he has continually tracked the trail of the beast into the holy of holies—but only because it hurt him so much to find it there.

J. W. Krutch, "Modern Love and Modern Fiction"

If there are plenty of good scientific and technological reasons—ectogenesis, cloning, serial mass production, TV—why *Brave New World* could not have been written before it was, there are also some very good literary reasons. For *Brave New World* is, literarily speaking, a very modern book; modern not only because it deals frankly with a typically "modern" subject like sex, but modern in the very ways it conceives of and presents its subject and characters.

There are in *Brave New World* no long introductory descriptions of landscape or environment in the Victorian or Edwardiam manner; there is, initially, no attempt to give more than a very

13

rudimentary outline of the physical and psychological traits of the characters. There is no elaborate explanation of how we came to be where we are, nor even at first an explanation at all why we are where we are: six-hundred-odd years in the future. The starting assumption is simply that it is quite normal to be in a big factory in the middle of London. Only gradually and indirectly does that assumption also become startling, as it becomes clear to us what the products of this factory are and what kind of a world we have entered.

This technique of indirection is one that Virginia Woolf ascribes, in "Mr. Bennett and Mrs. Brown" (1924), to the moderns. For her—and by extension for the modern novelist—the way to get at the heart of a character and a situation is not to add up every item of information we can gather about them; the whole is not to be found in the summing up of all of the parts. That way lies dullness—and Arnold Bennett. The better way is to try to get at the whole by being, as it were, paradoxically content with the part. To get at the essence of Mrs. Brown—Woolf's hypothetical example—we need to be told nothing directly of her history and background; we merely need to overhear her conversation in a railway compartment for an hour or so. Out of the apparently random odds and ends of this conversation, we can, by an act of the imagination, reconstruct her life and penetrate her soul.

What happens when a modern novelist resolves to transfer a Mrs. Brown or any other person into a work of fiction is that, inevitably, the author himself more or less disappears; the reader is left alone, seemingly at least, with the character(s). The modern novel therefore involves a shift of responsibility for character and situation away from the author and toward the reader, who must reach his conclusions about both "unaided." This is clearly what happens in Virginia Woolf's own novels, or in the novels of other modern writers like Waugh, Bowen, Isherwood—and Huxley.

This is not to say that Huxley or Isherwood or anyone else read Woolf and then decided to write a new kind of novel. Woolf is merely, as she knew full well herself, making explicit theoretically a conclusion that she had noted in practice for some years, in Joyce and others. Huxley himself had employed this new and modern manner from the very outset of his career in stories like "The

Farcical History of Richard Greenow" (1918) and novels like *Crome Yellow* (1921).

The first three chapters of *Brave New World*, especially, are masterfully composed in the indirect manner. Very little is heard; almost everything is overheard. To this manner Huxley also adds a refinement of his own devising, a technique perhaps best called "counterpoint," since Huxley had used it most fully before in *Point Counter Point* (1929), though there are intimations of it as early as *Those Barren Leaves* (1925). This technique involves a simultaneous juxtaposition of different elements of the narrative, much as musical counterpoint means sounding different notes simultaneously with a *cantus firmus*. The result in music is—or should be—a complex harmony; in Huxley's fiction the result is, usually, a complex dissonance, a subtle and often brilliant cacophony of ironies. The third chapter of *Brave New World* is set up entirely in this kind of counterpoint, gathering together the various narrative strains of the first two chapters and juxtaposing them without any editorial comment, slowly at first and then with gathering momentum, climaxing in a crescendo that fuses snatches of Mond's lecture, Lenina's conversation with Fanny, Henry Foster's with Benito Hoover, Bernard Marx's resentful thoughts, and bits of hypnopaedic wisdom.

The result is astonishing and far more effective in drawing us into the noisy and frantically joyless atmosphere of the new world state than pages of descriptive writing would have been. It is one of the most remarkable pieces of writing in the modern British novel.

Brave New World is modern, too, in another literary respect. It is shot through with literary allusions. Most of these allusions— such as the title and much of the conversation of the Savage—are to Shakespeare, but there are also more or less direct or indirect allusions to Shaw, Wells, T. S. Eliot, D. H. Lawrence, Voltaire, Rousseau, Thomas Gray, and Dante. The point of these allusions is not, I think, to show how clever and sophisticated and knowledgeable a writer Aldous Huxley is; the point is, rather, as in the poetry of T. S. Eliot—or Huxley's own poetry, for that matter—to reveal ironically the inadequacies of the present (or the present as contained in the future) by comparing it with the past. This is primarily how the literary allusions function in *The Waste Land* or

in "Whispers of Immortality"—from which Huxley derives
Lenina's peculiarly pneumatic sexuality—and that is also how they
function primarily in *Brave New World*.[1] The juxtaposition of
Cleopatra with a bored modern woman who has nothing to do or of
Spenser's and Goldsmith's lovers with the dreary amorous adventures of a modern secretary serves the same purpose as the juxtaposition of the love of Othello and Desdemona with that of the
hero and heroine of the "feely" "Three Weeks in a Helicopter," or
even the love of Romeo and Juliet with that of Lenina and the
Savage. The effect in both cases is that of a literary double expo-
sure, which provides a simultaneous view of two quite distinct and
yet horribly similar realities. The tension between the two—that
which pulls them violently apart and at the same time pushes them
violently together—produces a powerful irony, which is just what
Eliot and Huxley want to produce. By means of this irony it then
becomes possible for Huxley, or the "narrator" of his novel, to
guide the reader's response without seeming to do so, without
requiring any overt interference on his part. By merely hinting, for
example, at the analogy between the Fordian state and Prospero's
island, Huxley manages to convey ironically a disapproval of that
state without ever having to voice it himself. And he can safely
leave it to the reader to make the rest of the ironic identification:
Mond is Prospero; Lenina is Miranda; the Savage is Ferdinand;
Bernard Marx is Caliban. Or, if one prefers, Mond is a kind of
Prospero and Alonso combined; the Savage, as befits his name, is
Caliban, and his mother, Linda, is Sycorax; Lenina is a perverse
Miranda and Bernard a strange Ferdinand. Or, to give another
twist to it, the Director of Hatcheries and Conditioning is a kind of
Alonso who abandoned Linda and John to the desert; they in turn
are, respectively, Prospero and Miranda, with their sexes re-
versed; the Indians and especially Popé are a kind of collective
Caliban; Lenina, the aggressive lover, is a female Ferdinand, and
Bernard a sort of rescuing Ariel. The same kind of ironic game can
be played with *Romeo and Juliet* and *Othello*. In this way the
ironies multiply until they become mind-boggling.[2]

This is not to say that there is no direct narrative guidance in
Huxley's novel. The reader is explicitly told, for example, that
mental excess has produced in Helmholtz Watson's character the
same results as a physical defect has in Bernard Marx. Or Bernard's

psyche is analyzed for us in terms of an inferiority complex that finds its chief victims in his friends rather than his enemies. These are all acts of narrative interference and by no means isolated ones, but even so they are kept in the background and are, generally speaking, confined to attempts to make the psychological functioning of the characters more comprehensible.

Brave New World is a novel that is very carefully planned and put together. As Donald Watt has recently shown in his study of Huxley's revisions in the typescript of *Brave New World,* a number of the best stylistic effects and one of the best scenes—the soma distribution riot—were afterthoughts, inserted by Huxley after he had finished the rest of the novel.[3] This is not unusual for Huxley, who always revised his work thoroughly and in the process often came up with some of his best ideas. Just when Huxley started work on the novel is, however, not clear, though it is certain that the novel was finished, except for a few final touches, by the end of August 1931. *Brave New World* is first mentioned, though not by name, in Huxley's correspondence on May 18, 1931, and about a week later he wrote to his brother, Julian, that "all I've been writing during the last month won't do and I must re-write in quite another way" (L, 348–49). This clearly means that Huxley must have started the novel no later than the end of April or the beginning of May 1931. There is, however, some evidence to suggest that he may have been planning and perhaps even writing *Brave New World* as early as the latter part of 1930. For in an essay published in January 1931, entitled "Boundaries of Utopia," Huxley describes a future world that in general—and in some striking details—anticipates the new world state. "Served by mechanical domestics," Huxley writes in this essay, "exploiting the incessant labour of mechanical slaves, the three-hundred-a-year men of the future state will enjoy an almost indefinite leisure. A system of transport, rapid, frequent and cheap [taxicopters and passenger rockets], will enable him to move about the globe more freely than the emigrant *rentier* of the present age. . . . The theatres in which the egalitarians will enjoy the talkies, tasties, smellies, and feelies, the Corner Houses where they will eat their synthetic poached eggs on toast-substitute and drink their substitutes of coffee, will be prodigiously much vaster and more splendid than anything we know today." Huxley concludes the essay by asserting that continuous progress is possible only on condition that the size of the population be limited and genetically improved.[4]

The focus on leisure, rapid transport, amusements, synthetic substitutes, and genetic improvements in humans all suggest close links with *Brave New World*, so close indeed that it is difficult to believe that the novel was not already germinating in Huxley's mind and perhaps even on his typewriter. If this is true, then Huxley spent the better part of a year—nine or ten months— writing and rewriting *Brave New World*. If it is not true, then Huxley must have planned and written the novel in the astonishingly short time of a little less than four months. In either case, it is a remarkable achievement in a remarkably short time, though it should be remembered that utopian and anti-utopian ideas had been floating through Huxley's mind and popping up occasionally in his fiction since as early as 1921.[5] However short a time the actual writing may have taken, there were clearly years of general preparation and preliminary thought that went into the novel.

One of the chief problems Huxley had with *Brave New World*, according to Donald Watt, was with the characters. On the evidence of the revisions, Watt concludes that Huxley seems first to have thought of making Bernard Marx the rebellious hero of the novel but then changed his mind and deliberately played him down into a kind of anti-hero. After rejecting the possibility of a heroic Bernard, Huxley next seems to have turned to the Savage as an alternative. According to Watt, there are in the typescript several indications, later revised or omitted, of the Savage's putting up or at least planning to put up violent resistance to the new world state, perhaps even of leading a kind of revolution against it. But in the process of rewriting the novel, Huxley also abandoned this idea in favor of having no hero at all, or of having only the vague adumbration of a hero in Helmholtz Watson.[6]

Watt's analysis of the revisions in *Brave New World* is very helpful and interesting; he shows convincingly, I think, that Huxley was unable to make up his mind until very late in the composition of the novel just what direction he wanted the story and the leading male characters to take. From this uncertainty, however, I do not think it necessary to leap to the further conclusion that Huxley had difficulty in creating these characters themselves. Huxley's supposedly inadequate ability to create living characters, the result of his not being a "congenital novelist," is a question that often arises in discussions of his fiction, and in connection with longer and more traditionally novelistic novels like *Point Counter Point* or *Eyeless in Gaza* (1936) appropriately so. But *Brave New World* is anything but a traditional novel in this sense. It is not a novel of character but a relatively short satirical tale, a "fable," much like Voltaire's *Candide*. One hardly demands fully developed and "round" characters of *Candide*, nor should one of *Brave New World*.

This is all the more the case because the very nature of the new world state precludes the existence of fully developed characters. Juliets and Anna Kareninas, or Hamlets and Prince Vronskys, are by definition impossibilities in the new world state. To ask for them is to ask for a different world, the very world whose absence Huxley's novel so savagely laments. Character, after all, is shaped by suffering, and the new world state has abolished suffering in favor of a continuous, soma-stupefied, infantile "happiness." In such an environment it is difficult to have characters who grow and develop and are "alive."

Despite all this, it is surprising and noteworthy how vivid and even varied Huxley's characters are. With all their uniformly standardized conditioning, Alphas and Betas turn out to be by no means alike: the ambitious "go-getter" Henry Foster is different from his easy-going friend Benito Hoover; the unconventional and more "pneumatic" Lenina Crowne from the moralistic and rather less pneumatic Fanny Crowne; the resentful and ugly Bernard Marx from the handsome and intelligent Helmholtz Watson. Huxley, in fact, seems to work consistently and consciously in terms of contrastive/complementary pairs to suggest various possibilities of response to similar situations. So, too, Helmholtz and the Savage are another pair, as are the Savage and Mond, Mond and the DHC, Bernard and Henry Foster. The most fully developed instance of this pairing or doubling technique is the trip that Bernard and Lenina make to the Indian reservation, a trip that duplicates the one made some years earlier by the DHC and a "particularly pneumatic" Beta-Minus named Linda. Like the DHC, Bernard also leaves Lenina, another pneumatic Beta, (briefly) behind while returning to civilization, and during this interval she, too, is lusted after by a savage, much as Popé and the other Indians lust after

Linda. Even the novel as a whole reveals a similar sort of doubling structure, with the new world state on the one hand and the Indian reservation on the other.

Within limits, the characters, even some of the minor and superficial characters like Henry Foster, are capable of revealing other and deeper facets of their personality. Returning with Lenina from the Stoke Poges Obstacle Golf Course, Henry Foster's helicopter suddenly shoots upward on a column of hot air rising from the Slough Crematorium.[7] Lenina is delighted at this brief switchback, but "Henry's tone was almost, for a moment, melancholy. 'Do you know what that switchback was?' he said. 'It was some human being finally and definitely disappearing. Going up in a squirt of hot gas. It would be curious to know who it was—a man or a woman, an Alpha or an Epsilon . . .'" (62). Henry quickly jolts himself out of this atypical mood and reverts to his normally obnoxious cheerfulness, but for an instant at least there was a glimpse of a real human being.

Much more than Henry, Bernard Marx and Helmholtz Watson are capable of complexity of response. The latter especially and partly through his contact with the Savage grows increasingly aware of himself as a separate human entity and of his dissatisfaction with the kind of life he had led hitherto. As an Emotional Engineer and contriver of slogans, Helmholtz has been very successful, as he also has been in the capacities of lover and sportsman; but he despises this success and seeks for a satisfaction for which he has no name and which he can only dimly conceive. He comes closest to expressing it in the poem that eventually leads to his exile, the poem in which an ideal and absent woman becomes more real to him—in the manner of Mallarmé's flower that is absent from all bouquets—than any woman he has ever actually met.

In the end Helmholtz agrees to being sent into frigid exile in the Falkland Islands. The reason he chooses such a place rather than possible alternatives like Samoa or the Marquesas is because there he will not only have solitude but also a harsh climate in which to suffer and to gain new and very different experiences. His aim, however, is not, as some critics have suggested, to seek mystic experience;[8] he simply wants to learn how to write better poetry. "I should like a thoroughly bad climate," he tells Mustapha Mond. "I believe one would write better if the climate were bad. If there were a lot of wind and storms for example . . ." (187–88). This hardly represents a search for mysticism and God; in this novel only the Savage, and he in only a very qualified way, can be described as seeking after such ends. Helmholtz merely wants more and better words. In the context of Huxley's work, he harks back to a character like Denis Stone in *Crome Yellow,* not forward to the pacifist Anthony Beavis in *Eyeless in Gaza* or in the inner-directed Propter in *After Many a Summer* (1939).

The same is true of Bernard Marx. Despite the apparent fact that Huxley once had more exalted intentions for him, Bernard belongs very much to the familiar Huxleyan category of the anti-hero, best exemplified perhaps by Theodore Gumbril, Jr., the so-called Complete Man of *Antic Hay* (1923). Like Gumbril, Bernard is able to envision and even seek after a love that is not merely sexual, but, like Gumbril again, his search is half-hearted. He is willing to settle for less because it is so much easier than trying to strive for more. Bernard is weak and cowardly and vain, much more so than Gumbril, and this makes him an unsympathetic character in a way that Gumbril is not. Nevertheless Bernard is undoubtedly capable of seeing the better, even if in the end he follows the worse.

Bernard is certainly a more fully developed character than Helmholtz; he is, in fact, with the exception of the Savage, the character about whom we know most in the entire novel. Just why this should be so is a question worth asking, just as it is worth asking why Bernard is the first of the novel's three malcontents to be brought to our attention.[9]

Bernard's importance resides, I think, in his incapacity. The stability of the new world state can be threatened, it is clear, from above and from below. In the case of Helmholtz the threat is from above, from a surfeit of capacity; in Bernard's case it is from below, from a lack of sufficient capacity. This is not simply to say that Bernard is more stupid than Helmholtz, which he probably is, but rather that because of his physical inferiority he has developed a compulsive need to assert his superiority. It is this incapacity which, paradoxically, seems to make Bernard the more dangerous threat, for it compels him to rise to a position of power in his society; he wants to be accepted by his society, but only on his own terms, terms that are not acceptable in the long run if stability is to be maintained. Helmholtz, on the other hand, is a loner who really wants to have nothing to do with the society at all, and in this sense he represents much less of a threat. The Savage, on the other hand, though most violent and uncompromising in his hatred of and desire to destroy the new world state, is really no threat at all, for he originates from outside the society and is a kind of *lusus naturae*. There is never likely to be another Savage, but it is very probable that there will be or that there are more Bernards and Helmholtzes.

Both Bernard and Helmholtz are fairly complex characters. What is surprising, however, is that the same is true of Lenina Crowne. She seems at first to be nothing more than a pretty and addle-brained young woman without any emotional depth whatever. And at first it is true that this is all she is; but she changes in the course of the novel into something quite different. She changes because she falls in love.

The great irony of Lenina's falling in love is that she does not realize what it is that has happened to her; like Helmholtz she has no name for the new feeling and hence no way of conceiving or understanding what it is. She can only think of love in the physiological ways in which she has been conditioned to think of it; but her feeling is different.

So subtle is Huxley's portrayal of the change in Lenina that, as far as I know, no critic has ever commented on it. Yet Lenina is clearly predisposed from the very beginning to a love relationship that is not sanctioned by her society. As we learn from her conversation with Fanny, Lenina has been going with Henry Foster for four months without having had another man, and this in defiance of what she knows to be the properly promiscuous code of sexual behavior. When Fanny takes her up on this point of unconventionality, Lenina reacts almost truculently and replies that she "jolly well [does not] see why there should have been" anyone other than Henry (32). Her inability to see this error in her sexual ways is what predisposes her for the much greater and more intense feeling that she develops for the Savage.

The stages of her growing love for the Savage and her increasing mystification at what is happening within herself are handled with a brilliantly comic touch. There is the scene following Lenina's and the Savage's return from the feelies when the Savage sends her off in the taxicopter just as she is getting ready to seduce him. There is the touching moment when Lenina, who had once been terrified of pausing with Bernard to look at the sea and the moon over the Channel, now lingers "for a moment to look at the moon," before being summoned by an irritated and uncomprehending Arch-Songster (144). There is Lenina's increasing impatience with the obtuseness of Henry Foster and his blundering solicitousness. There are the fond murmurings to herself of the Savage's name. There is the conference with Fanny as to what she should do about the Savage's strange coldness toward her. There is her blunt rejection of Fanny's advice to seek consolation with one of the millions of other men. There is the wonderful scene in which she seeks out the Savage alone in his apartment, discovers to her amazement that he loves her, sheds her clothing, and receives, to her even greater amazement, insults, blows, and a threat to kill. There is the final terrible scene at the lighthouse when Lenina steps out of the helicopter, looks at the Savage with "an uncertain, imploring, almost abject smile," and then "pressed both hands to her left side [i.e., to her heart], and on that peach-bright, doll-beautiful face of hers appeared a strangely incongruous expression of yearning distress. Her blue eyes seemed to grow larger, brighter; and suddenly two tears rolled down her cheeks" (211). Again the Savage attacks her, this time with his whip, maddened by desire, by remorse, and by the horde of obscenely curious sightseers. In the end, however, desire triumphs and the Savage and Lenina consummate their love in an orgy-porgian climax. When the Savage awakens to the memory of what has happened, he knows he cannot live with such defilement. For him the end is swift and tragic. For Lenina, however, there is no end; her tragedy—and for all the comedy and irony in which her love for the Savage is immersed, the word *tragedy* is not entirely inappropriate—her tragedy is that she has felt an emotion that she can never express or communicate or realize again.

The characters of *Brave New World*, it is safe to conclude, are not merely made of cardboard and *papier-mâché*. That they are nonetheless not full and complete human beings is quite true; but for all the technology and conditioning and impulses toward uniformity, there is still something profoundly human about them. As Lenina's development in the novel indicates, it is possible, as it were, to scratch the plasticized "doll-like" surface of a citizen—at least of an Alpha or Beta citizen—of the new world state and draw actual blood. In this sense and to this degree, Huxley's vision of the perfectly planned future is not without hope; for all the genetic engineering and conditioning, basic humanity remains much the same as it always was. Its imperfections and its needs, even under such greatly altered conditions, inevitably reappear. And it is for this reason, I think, that Huxley's vision is so extraordinarily powerful and compelling; because in the people he portrays we can still somehow recognize ourselves.

Even in the lower "bokanovskified" castes, humanity will sometimes succeed in breaking through the hard shell of genetics and conditioning. We catch a glimpse of this humanity in the apelike figure of an Epsilon-Minus Semi-Moron elevator operator:

> "Roof!"
> He flung open the gates. The warm glory of afternoon sunlight made him start and blink his eyes. "Oh, roof!" he repeated in a voice of rapture. He was as though suddenly and joyfully awakened from a dark annihilating stupor. "Roof!"
> He smiled up with a kind of doggily expectant adoration into the faces of his passengers. Talking and laughing together, they stepped out into the light. The liftman looked after them.
> "Roof?" he said once more, questioningly.
> Then a bell rang, and from the ceiling of the lift a loud-speaker began, very softly and yet very imperiously, to issue its commands.
> "Go down," it said, "go down. Floor Eighteen. Go down, go down. Floor Eighteen. Go down, go . . ."
> The liftman slammed the gates, touched a button and instantly dropped back into the drawing twilight of the well, the twilight of his own habitual stupor. (P. 49)

This vignette—which incidentally resembles very closely one of Huxley's earliest poems, "Mole"—pathetically reveals how impossible it is, even under "ideal" technological conditions and even with the stupidest of humans, to block out all knowledge of a different and better reality. The vignette, like the poem it evokes, functions symbolically as well. The almost subhuman elevator operator ferries the seeming "men-like-gods" upward toward the bright heavens, into which they will depart with their helicopters, while he himself reverts once more to the infernal depths. But he does not and cannot know—and herein lies the irony—that they too are inhabitants of a genetically engineered and conditioned limbo only a little larger and better lit than the dim shaft through which he drops.

The new world state uses all its power to shield its citizens from the intimations of any reality other than that which they are conditioned to perceive. Bright lights and electric advertisements hide the night, and continuous noise drowns out any possible silence. Even after the lights are switched off and the Sixteen Sexophonists stop playing, there is no need to confront the silent darkness because, although "the depressing stars had travelled quite some way across the heavens" and "the separating screen of sky-signs had now to a great extent dissolved," Lenina and Henry Foster "still retained their happy ignorance of the night," protected as they are by soma. Soma has raised "a quite impenetrable wall between the actual universe and their minds" (64). Though supposedly without side-effects, soma, like other drugs, leads to "highs" that end up being very low.

The greatest triumphs in obscuring the dark truths are achieved by the new world state through death conditioning. Children are brought to the beds of the dying and these beds are surrounded by TV's, continuous musak, and perfume. Meanwhile the dying are pumped blissfully full of soma. In this way death is deprived both of its sting and of its victory. It becomes just another event like Obstacle-Golf.

Still, occasionally the night creeps in, over the English Channel or in the switchback above the Slough Crematorium; the inner and outer shields of the new world state, powerful though they may be, are not perfect. This is true also of the past. History, in Our Ford's words, is officially bunk; all the old books have either been destroyed or securely locked away in Mustapha Mond's safe, but even so remnants of the past stubbornly survive. They survive in a kind of subculture whose existence is not officially recognized though it is assumed as self-evident by officials like the DHC and Mustapha Mond. The words *father* and *mother*, for example, are obscenities in the new world state, but it is clear that virtually every citizen has heard these words before and knows what they mean. Such knowledge is only possible if the past, bunk or no bunk, has survived, if people are aware that once there were families and society was very differently organized.[10]

The very plot of the novel concerns the imperfections of the supposedly "perfect" state. Or, rather, the plots, for the novel really has two plots more or less coterminous with each other: the first, which deals with the deviant behavior of Bernard Marx and Helmholtz Watson, two rebels who seek to escape solidarity and assert their individuality; and the second, which recounts the love story of the Savage and Lenina. These two plots are, of course, interconnected, and indeed the relationship between Bernard and Lenina to some extent serves to anticipate the fuller and more dramatic relationship between Lenina and the Savage, just as the extreme individuality of the Savage serves to contrast with and complement the individuality of Bernard and Helmholtz. The crucial element in both plots, the element that in both cases precipitates the climax, is the Savage.

The Savage is the most important single character in the novel. We know more about his background—partly because he has more background to know about—and more about his psyche than those of any other character. Though not the hero of the novel in the sense that he is presented as a practical alternative to new world man, he is unquestionably more fully and profoundly human than anyone else, including Helmholtz. His life is heroic and his death tragic, even though he may strike us as comically naive in his misapprehension of Lenina or even downright insane in the ferocity of his religious mania. But then King Lear or Othello are also extraordinarily naive and arguably mad, as well as undeniably heroic. Normality and sanity are not necessary criteria for heroism or tragedy.

The Savage is the most important character in the novel and he is also the most puzzling. There are a multitude of reasons why Huxley should have wished to include such a character in *Brave New World*, reasons that have to do with D. H. Lawrence's "Dark God," Rousseau and Chateaubriand's "noble savage," or even Voltaire's *Candide*, in which there is a character named "L'Ingénu," a twenty-year-old French nobleman who was raised by the Huron Indians, who has read only Rabelais and parts of Shakespeare (which, however, he knows by heart), and who turns out to be very attractive to the jaded ladies of Paris.[11] Good as all these reasons may be, they still do not explain why the Savage must be a savage, why, for example, he cannot simply be a "normal" twentieth-century man. To be sure, it would have been extremely difficult for Huxley to import a remnant of such an earlier but still technologically fairly advanced period into his future world; to do so he would have had to resort, as Wells did, to unlikely devices like time-travel or Rip Van Winkle-like slumbers. Even so, it would have been possible, for example, for Huxley to introduce a descendant of one of the many exiles from the new world state; in this way he could have presented an alternative to that state in a sense that the Savage and the Indian reservation do not do so. This is in fact pretty much what Huxley does in *Island*.

The reason why Huxley does not present such an alternative, one is forced to conclude, is that he does not wish to. Huxley himself admits as much in his 1946 foreword to *Brave New World*. "At the time the book was written," he says, "this idea, that human beings are given free will to choose between insanity on the one hand and lunacy on the other, was one that I found amusing and regarded as quite possibly true" (viii). But this still leaves partly unanswered the question why the Savage must be savage, and why he must occupy so prominent a position in the novel.

The answer, I think, lies in the fact that the Savage is savage—but in temperament, not in culture. Culturally he is, in fact, no savage at all, but more civilized than any other character in the novel, except perhaps Mustapha Mond. His reading of Shakespeare and his exclusion from the Indian pueblo society have forced him to turn inward upon his own psychological resources, and this has made of him an emotionally rich, sensitive, and cultivated person. Hence there is nothing barbaric about the Savage.

He is, however, savage in his rejection of the comforts, the superficiality, and the moral laxity of the new world state. He is full of emotional power and intensity, ready to do quixotic battle against the faceless new world and its police; ready to reject out of hand any of the temptations which that Satanic materialist, Mustapha Mond, may offer him. The Savage is, finally, the man of spirit, in both senses of that word: he has courage and soul; he is the man of spirit opposed to the man of sense, again in both meanings of the word: the man of sensuality and materialistic reason. Because he hovers between two societies—one that rejects him and the other that he rejects—he is that unique phenomenon in both the Fordian and the Indian worlds: the man who is utterly alone. Not even the exiles are alone in the same sense, for no matter how isolated they may be, they are united in the knowledge that there are others like them. The Savage does not have this knowledge to fall back on. The only companion he has is God, and God is the last being he addresses and the last word he speaks before his suicide.

This final desperate act with which the novel concludes is the act of a madman, so twisted by his guilt at his mother's death, so tortured by the strange mixture of fatalistic *penitente*-ism and Shakespearean idealism, that he cannot cope with the other, less spiritual and idealistic selves that also dwell within him. In the final stage of his existence, the Savage turns into a kind of monk who withdraws into the desert. There, like St. Anthony before him, he is confronted and tempted by visions of lust and sinfulness, visions that, like St. Anthony again, require all the strength of his will— and his whip—to withstand.[12] In the end, he can withstand no longer.

The death he confers upon himself is not admirable, but it is by no means trivial or ridiculous. It is an individual death, one brought on by an intense desire to be more and greater than he is, and by his savage disappointment at realizing that it cannot be. But in the end the Savage's tragic failure leaves us with the feeling, at least, that it is better and nobler to try to be more than human and fail, than to try to be less than human and succeed.

The Savage, then, ironically is the civilized man who is unable to exist in a world in which civilization is defined as savagery. He is the final heir of that great tradition in Western culture which finds its values not in the greatest happiness of the greatest number, but in the greatest sensitivity of the limited and often lonely individual. To make such a figure embodying such a tradition the hero of his novel may seem paradoxical for a writer like Huxley, who in the twenties enjoyed a reputation for being hypermodern, for this is a tradition that reached its climax in the nineteenth century. But then Huxley, like Shaw and many another "modern," is really an inheritor and passer-on of the values of that century. It is the century, after all, that transformed the Savage's Shakespeare from an entertaining dramatist into the greatest poet—and perhaps therefore greatest man—who ever lived, and that opposed the supposedly scientific ethics of Jeremy Bentham with Arnoldian sweetness and light. For the Savage and for Huxley, as for John Ruskin, there is ultimately no wealth but Life, but Life in capital letters, not mere existence, not mere pullulation. It is the tradition that, more forcefully than anyone else, was expressed—and lived—by another great modern, D. H. Lawrence, who hated the masses and the machines and the science that presumed to make those masses "happy."

Looking back at his novel after a lapse of fifteen years, Huxley once suggested (what should really be obvious to everyone and what differentiates this novel so radically from vaguely similar but inferior works by other authors) that the theme of *Brave New World* is "not the advancement of science as such; it is the advancement of science as it affects human individuals" (1946 foreword to *Brave New World*, p. x). This is a problem that had been growing increasingly acute since the great scientific avalanche of the late nineteenth and early twentieth centuries (hence Helmholtz, Bernard, and Watson as names for some of the main characters in the novel), and which, after the First World War and the Soviet Revolution, had assumed ever more oppressive political and economic forms (therefore Lenina, Marx, and Mond).

The intensity with which Huxley felt *Brave New World* to be an attack on the present or on the present as contained in the future can be seen from his repeated attempts to gauge the progress of the malady of dehumanization. When he took its temperature in an article written for *Life* magazine in 1948, the great blights of fascism, the Second World War, and the atom bomb had intervened to alter the condition of mankind and therefore Huxley's diagnosis. Now he maintained that, instead of one, there were two myths underlying the psyche and behavior of Western man. To the myth of progress he added the myth of nationalism, the former promulgated through the medium of advertising, the latter through political propaganda and brainwashing.[13] From this we can see—though Huxley did not explicitly make the connection—that in the new world the myth of nationalism with its accompanying propaganda has disappeared because of the massive destruction of the Nine Years' War (as Mustapha Mond instructs the Savage) and because the instruments of technological blandness have triumphed over those of nationalistic brutality; indeed, part of the plot of the novel consists of a reenactment of this triumph in miniature. On the other hand, in *Ape and Essence* (1948), which Huxley was working on as he wrote the *Life* essay, it is apparent that the myth of progress has been displaced by a religious variant of nationalism. The stupidity of both of these myths, according to Huxley, is that they stress the external aspects of life, not the internal. Their disciples, therefore, must inevitably "progress" to one or another kind of perdition: the perdition of "heaven" or the perdition of hell. Hence this kind of progress is really no progress at all. Real progress, in Huxley's terms, can only be defined as "personal progress," or "internal progress." It is only through this type of advancement that one can hope to create a "genuinely human society," and only such a society can assure the continued existence of genuine human individuals, not diabolically happy or diabolically unhappy animals.

As I have already suggested, the idea for the novel that was later to become *Brave New World* had germinated in Huxley's mind a decade earlier. In *Crome Yellow* (1921), Scogan, a verbose and parasitical materialist, outlines for the benefit of Denis Stone, the hero and something of a romantic idealist, his plan for the "Rational State." In this state, psychologists would examine all children and separate them into three distinct categories: a small number of Directing Intelligences, a larger number of Men of Faith, and the vast mass of the Herd. The first class, the only one capable of thought and able to achieve even a "certain degree of freedom," would use the men of faith or action to govern the state and the herd. To ensure that this last class would carry out its appointed tasks dutifully and uncomplainingly, the Intelligences would devise and the Men of Faith would apply suitable mechanisms of conditioning: "In the upbringing of the Herd," Scogan ecstatically concludes, "humanity's almost boundless suggestibility will be scientifically exploited. Systematically, from earliest infancy, its members will be assured that there is no happiness to be found except in work and obedience; they will be made to believe that they are happy, that they are tremendously important beings, and that everything they do is noble and significant. For the lower species the earth will be restored to the center of the universe and man to pre-eminence on the earth. Oh, I envy the lot of the commonalty in the Rational State! Working their eight hours a day, obeying their betters, convinced of their own grandeur and significance and immortality, they will be marvellously happy, happier than any race of men has ever been. They will go through life in a rosy state of intoxication, from which they will never awake. The Men of Faith will play the cupbearers at this lifelong bacchanal, filling and ever filling again with the warm liquor that the Intelligences, in sad and sober privacy behind the scenes, will brew for the intoxication of the subjects" (*Crome Yellow*, 164).

After Scogan ends this hymn of praise to the bacchanalian Rational State, Denis Stone naturally inquires what his place might be in the new order. The question is a difficult one for Scogan, but he answers it with impeccable logic. Since Denis, a poet, would be unfit for manual labor, since he is clearly not a man of faith, and since he has not the "marvellously clear and merciless and penetrating" rational faculty of the Directing Intelligences, he would have to be consigned to the lethal chamber.

Scogan's Rational State, despite its cruelty, still permits a certain measure of freedom to an entire class of citizens. The intellectuals, within limits, can still be aware of reality and of themselves as individuals. Not so the citizens of the new world, for they are almost universally condemned to standardized thoughts and emotions. It is this difference which most clearly distinguishes the brave new world of A.D. 1932 (or A.F. 632) from the hypothetical Rational State of 1922—and it is a difference that is due, apparently, to Huxley's intervening encounter with America and the "American Civilization."

In 1926 Huxley made a trip around the world, traveling eastward and stopping primarily in India, Burma, Malaya, and the United States, paying his bills by writing up his experiences for British and American papers. Later in the same year he collected these fragments and joined them together into *Jesting Pilate*, a fascinating travelogue of a man in search of the truth but too pressed to stay for a definite answer—but not too pressed to await and formulate provisional ones, such as the "truth" (which was later to become a massive lie for the author of *Island*) that the ways of the East were not noticeably superior to those of Europe, or the "truth" that Western culture in its westernmost or Californian manifestations boded ill for the future of mankind.

In a special section of *Jesting Pilate* entitled "Los Angeles, A Rhapsody," Huxley records his impressions of the City of Dreadful Joy, or more briefly, the Joy City, with devastating irony. Los Angeles, as Huxley perceives it, is a city in which everybody is happy but no one is quite sure why, where there is hectic activity on all sides, with people rushing to and fro in their automobiles, bombarded by advertising and enticed by entertainment of every sort, from religious to alcoholic, but where there is hardly any trace of intellectual life or purpose. Here man, as in the future new world, is created for the good time, not the good time for man, with the inescapable consequence that his soul and body become standardized. The women, for example, are "plumply ravishing" and give promise (as do their equivalents in the newer world) of "pneumatic bliss," but of not much else, to judge by their uniform, unindividual, and blank faces. For Huxley, it is plain, there is no need to travel into the future to find the brave new world; it already exists, only too palpably, in the American Joy City, where the declaration of dependence begins and ends with the single-minded pursuit of happiness.

Typically "American," too, is the rejection of everything old. "History," Mustapha Mond remarks, citing one of the prime commandments of Our Ford, "is bunk." And not just written history or old books—Shakespeare and the Bible, which have to be locked away in a safe—but all old ideas and institutions are bunk. The very concept of age is bunk for those who live "modern" in the soma generation. How horrified the orthodox Fordians are by the unexpected appearance of a woman who reveals her actual age in wrinkles, sagging breasts, and flabby flesh; and how disgusted even that woman herself is by her own condition, exiled though she has been from earthly paradise for more than two decades.[14]

The only adults who are permitted to influence the Fordian state are the ten so-called World Controllers, who function as a tiny priest class governing a vast population of blissfully ignorant babies. To judge by the example of Mustapha Mond, however, the World Controllers are a very sober and benevolent group who selflessly devote themselves to the welfare of their charges. Mond himself, as a former physicist of considerable promise, would have been happier pursuing his scientific researches undisturbed, but instead he chose the harder and less rewarding task of government.

It is on his own shoulders, and on those of his peers, that the ultimate responsibility for the operation of the Fordian state rests.

Though there is no religion in the new world beyond the materialistically oriented orgy-porgy services—sustained youth, as Mond observes to the Savage, allows one to be independent of God—the World Controllers seem fairly clearly to be modeled on the pope and cardinals of the Church of Rome. Like these, Mond is a father of his "children," guarding them from the burden and temptations of excessive knowledge and filling their lives with time-consuming pomp and circumstance. The Fordian state—even phrases like "Our Ford" or "Ford's in his flivver" imply it— resembles nothing so much as a secular theocracy.

That Huxley is fully conscious of this dimension of his satirical parable is implicit in the extended dialogue between Mond and Savage that occupies all of chapter 17. This chapter is a revision of the Grand Inquisitor episode in Dostoevski's *Brothers Karamazov,* with the roles of the Inquisitor and Christ reversed. Here it is the Christ-Savage who is indignant at the behavior of the Inquisitor-Controller and his presumption that man can live by soma alone. To be sure, unlike Dostoevski's Christ, Huxley's Controller does not maintain absolute silence in the face of his interlocutor's verbal onslaught, but he does the next best thing by seeking to overcome the Savage's objections through sweet reasonableness. Of course, like Christ he can afford to be tolerant, for he holds the supreme power in his hands: he rules over the godless utopia whose coming the Grand Inquisitor had foretold. That utopia exists—unlike Christ's heaven—not for the chosen few, who are in any event strong enough to help themselves, but for the masses of the weak and spineless, who do not know what to do with Christ's gift of freedom and who are only too pleased to rid themselves of the "terrible burden of that gift" in exchange for "being able to become a herd once again." The historical development of the Fordian world, as related by Mond, conforms strikingly to the pattern predicted by the Grand Inquisitor: "Oh, ages are yet to come of the confusion of free thought, of their science and cannibalism. For having begun to build their tower of Babel without us, they will end, of course with cannibalism. But then the beast will crawl to us and lick our feet and spatter them with tears of blood. . . . But then, and only then, the reign of peace and happiness will come for men. Thou art proud of Thine elect, but Thou hast only the elect, while we give rest to all. . . . With us all will be happy and will no more rebel nor destroy one another as under Thy freedom. Oh, we shall persuade them that they will become free when they renounce their freedom to us and submit to us" (238).[15] In its essential outlines, though not in its proportions and technological details, the new world matches the Grand Inquisitor's vision: "And all will be happy, all the millions of creatures except for the hundred thousand who rule over them. For only we, we who guard the mystery, shall be unhappy. There will be thousands of millions of happy ones and a hundred thousand sufferers who have taken upon themselves the curse of the knowledge of good and evil" (239).

Against this enforced happiness, the Savage asserts the "right to be unhappy," the right to deformity, to disease and suffering of all kinds, the right to endure pain and to limit pleasure. To Mustapha Mond, as to the Grand Inquisitor, the desire for and the exercise of such a right seem the only evils of which they can conceive. In the end, as in Ivan Karamazov's tale, one or the other "right" must triumph, and the other vanish utterly. It must be either soul or stomach, the love of God or the love of man: there is no other alternative.[16]

In the United States, especially in its westernmost parts, Huxley found incarnated most of the dream of the Grand Inquisitor, found the love of stomach and of mass man running rampant, and recognized that what confronted him here was the future of mankind. At the very beginning of "The Outlook for American Culture: Some Reflections in a Machine Age," as essay published in 1927, Huxley warned his readers that "speculating on the American future, we are speculating on the future of civilized man." One of the most ominous portents of the American way of life, Huxley went on the say, was that it embraced a large class of people who "do not want to be cultured, are not interested in the higher life. For these people existence on the lower, animal levels is perfectly satisfactory. Given food, drink, and the company of their fellows, sexual enjoyment, and plenty of noisy distractions from without, they are happy." Furthermore, in America and the rest of the technologically advanced world, "all the resources of science are applied in order that imbecility may flourish and vulgarity cover the whole earth." The resources are so applied because quantity rather than quality is profitable for the capitalists involved: "The higher the degree of standardization in popular literature and art, the greater the profit for the manufacturer." All this mechanical and intellectual standardization, however, leads to the exaltation of the standardized man. It is this development that Huxley views with most concern: "This tendency to raise the ordinary, worldly man to the level of the extraordinary and disinterested one seems to me entirely deplorable. The next step will be to exalt him above the extraordinary man, who will be condemned and persecuted on principle because he is not ordinary—for not to be ordinary will be regarded as a crime. In this reversal of the old values I see a real danger, a menace to all desirable progress."[17]

It is this "next step" that has been taken in the Fordian (that is, American) world. For of all ideas, the idea of the extraordinary or individual person can least be tolerated by the new world. Extraordinary or individual behavior is a punishable offense.

The Savage is both extraordinary and an individual. His problem is that in neither society—the insane Indian or the lunatic Fordian—does any provision for such a being exist. Both societies have abolished individuality in order to become either subhumanly bestial or subhumanly mechanical. Both have paid far too high a price for social stability; and both, despite this stability, are consequently inferior to the unstable, unjust, unhappy, but still relatively human society of early twentieth-century Europe.

In the series of portraits of this twentieth-century society that Huxley had satirically sketched in his earlier novels, the fatal flaw was always the isolation of the individual. He was alone, trapped in his own conception of reality. This is not the case with the society of the new world, or, to a lesser degree, with that of the Indian *Penitentes*. In these societies the individual is solidly integrated, to the point of becoming an almost indistinguishable part of the whole. Too solidly, too indistinguishably—that is what is wrong with them. The price of social solidarity is the loss of individual existence. This is the paradox at the very heart of the novel: to be individual is to be isolated and unhappy; to be integrated is to be "happy," but happy in an inhuman fashion. It is the happiness, in the words of one of Huxley's early poems, of a "great goggling fish,"

or, as Mustapha Mond remarks, of being confined inside a bottle
whose walls exclude any reality and any awareness but that which
is allowed to filter through.

Huxley later came to consider the exclusion of no suitable alternative to piscine bliss or wretched individuality to be an artistic
fault of the novel. In his view, *Brave New World* should have
proposed another possibility, that of "sanity." In other words, it
should have described a community where "economics would be
decentralist and Henry-Georgian, politics Kropotkinesque and co-
operative"; where man would not be the slave of science and technology; where his religion would be "the conscious and intelligent
pursuit of man's Final End, the unitive knowledge of the Imma-
nent Tao or Logos, the transcendent God-head or Brahman"; and
where the prevailing philosophy of life would be "a kind of Higher
Utilitarianism, in which the Greatest Happiness principle would
be secondary to the Final End principle" (ix).

Thirty years after *Brave New World* Huxley fictionalized this
third possibility at length and in detail in *Island*. But even in *Brave
New World* itself some such possibility is already vaguely adum-
brated in the happy-unhappy islands to which Bernard and Helmholtz are finally exiled.

The central problem of *Brave New World* could also be phrased
in another way. The inhabitants of the Fordian state are aware
(insofar as they are aware of anything) of a reality that is totally
"happy"; the inhabitants of the Indian Reservation (including, for
the most part, the Savage), on the other hand, are aware only of a
sinister, "unhappy" reality. In neither society is there an awareness
of the whole truth, that is, of all realities—sinister, "happy," and
the multitude of intervening shadings; in fact, both are posited as a
negation of this whole truth. Both societies, consequently—and
the "individuals" they comprise—are imprisoned in their precon-
ceptions of reality and are essentially unaware. But unawareness of
the whole truth, as the novels up to and including *Point Counter
Point* (1928) indicated, leads either to individual isolation or to the
animality of the Complete Man; it does not lead to an integration
commensurate with true humanity. And it is precisely because
Brave New World, when measured against such a standard, is
found sorely wanting that it is a bitterly destructive satire.

2

The Future of Science and Our Freud

Future ages will bring with them new and probably unimagin-
ably great advances in this field of civilization and will increase
man's likeness to God still more.

Sigmund Freud, *Civilization
and Its Discontents*

The Old Vitalist, who was essentially a Materialist, has evolved
into the New Vitalist, who is, as every genuine scientist must
be, finally a metaphysician.

G. B. Shaw, preface to *Back
to Methuselah*

SCIENCE was in the Huxley blood. Or, if one wishes to be less
Lamarckian and more Lockean about it, in the Huxley air. Aldous
Huxley certainly had it from infancy and so did many another
offspring of Darwin's bulldog, his brother and half-brothers among
them. Before his partial blindness made it an absolute impossibil-
ity, Huxley had prepared himself for a career in biology, and
though he eventually became more than reconciled to being a
litterateur, the old hankering after strange scientific gods—and
devils—never left him. His essays bristle with scientific references
and in a small but significant way his two treatises on the effects of
psychedelic drugs, *The Doors of Perception* and *Heaven and Hell*,
along with the brief account of his experience of the Bates eye
treatment, *The Art of Seeing*, constitute scientific work. And, of
course, his novels and stories frequently seek to portray the
scientific mind, though rarely with the sympathy of the essays.

One recalls in particular the experimental biologists: Shearwater in *Antic Hay* and Lord Tantamount in *Point Counter Point;* the physicists; Einstein in *Ape and Essence* and Henry Maartens in *The Genius and the Goddess;* and the doctors: Miller in *Eyeless in Gaza*, Obispo in *After Many a Summer*, and McPhail in *Island*.

Huxley's most powerful rendering of the effects of science and technology, however, is unquestionably *Brave New World*. So deep a mark has this work left on the modern literate mind that the mere mention of it evokes a whole complex of hostile attitudes toward science. It has become a kind of byword for a society in which the values (or nonvalues) of scientific technology are dominant, and which has therefore reduced man to a species of machine. Swift and Butler and Morris and Tolstoy had denounced the machine before, but it was Huxley's ironic "Yes" that really began to awaken modern man to the horrible paradise of mechanical progress.

Like all successes, *Brave New World* has not lacked for literary foster fathers after the fact. At one time or another, all or part of the novel is alleged to have been derived (not to say plagarized) from Shakespeare, Dostoevski, Wells, Anatole France, Zamiatin, Joyce, or, in its scientific background, from J. B. S. Haldane and Bertrand Russell. While some of these claims are valid—especially in the case of the scientists—it is important to remember that *Brave New World* is more than an inspired pastiche. It is obvious that in a satire of this kind, some of the victims will be literary and will therefore reappear in distorted form, whereas in the matter of the scientific background, it is just as obvious that this must be drawn from somewhere, that it cannot be simply pulled out of thin air. Significantly, neither Haldane nor Russell (or for that matter Joyce or Wells) ever made even the slightest claim to have influenced the shape of *Brave New World*.[1]

Some of Huxley's science has, in the natural course of events, dated rather badly since the novel was first published some fifty-odd years ago. "One vast and obvious failure of foresight is immediately apparent," Huxley wrote in his 1946 foreword. "*Brave New World* contains no reference to nuclear fission" (x). The omission is actually, as he himself realized, rather surprising, since H. G. Wells had already described atomic bombs (using the very name) as early as 1914 in *The World Set Free*, on the basis of radium research carried out by Frederick Soddy. But is this really a "vast failure"? Almost certainly not. Huxley's satire, unlike the scientific romances of H. G. Wells, does not depend chiefly on lucky "hits" or unlucky misses. His aim is not so much to foresee what will happen to machines as to foresee what will happen to man. While granting that the development of machines has an undeniable effect on the development of man—a major contention of *Brave New World* anyway—it is still clear that mistakes in detail about the former do not necessarily vitiate general conclusions about the latter.

In any case, in the primary areas of his scientific interest (biology, physiology, and psychology) Huxley has dated practically not at all. His return trips to the Fordian society in *Brave New World Revisited* and, less extensively, in occasional letters and in essays like "Tomorrow and Tomorrow and Tomorrow" only confirmed him in his conclusions. Nor has subsequent research proved him wrong. On the contrary, Gordon Rattray Taylor warns us in *The Biological Time-Bomb* (1969) that "*Brave New World* is on its way,"[2] and in *Man and His Future* (1963) J. B. S. Haldane still views Huxley's biological forecasts as a definite possibility.[3] Gerald Leach's conclusion in *The Biocrats* (1970) that Huxley's scientific prophecies are not likely to be fulfilled is reached not on scientific but on social grounds.[4] In fact, Huxley's main argument that man is genetically modifiable and psychologically conditionable has, if anything, gained in scientific authority. Experiments, such as those in the cloning of vegetable matter by F. C. Seward, have raised the real, though still distant, prospect of human reproduction along lines similar to the "Bokanovsky process". And, of course, the pharmacological revolution of the last two decades has begun to deliver the actual means for chemical control of human behavior. *Brave New World*, it seems safe to say, is still highly relevant to any discussion of what may happen to mankind in the next few centuries. It may of course cease to be relevant—and let us hope that it will—but if so, it will probably be for political reasons, as George Orwell suggested, rather than for scientific ones.

How did Huxley manage to formulate a blueprint for the future that has remained so astonishingly accurate over so long a period? The answer to this question is extremely complex, as we shall see, and involves a consideration not merely of science, but of science fiction. It is complicated even further by the remarkable circumstance that *Brave New World* already existed, as we have seen, in embryo as early as 1921. In *Crome Yellow*, Scogan—whom T. S. Eliot identified with Bertrand Russell—envisions a future when "an impersonal generation will take the place of Nature's hideous system. In vast state incubators, rows upon rows of gravid bottles will supply the world with the population it requires. The family system will disappear—society, sapped at its very base, will have to find a new foundations: and Eros, beautifully and irresponsibly free, will flit like a gay butterfly from flower to flower through a sunlit world" (47). Later on, Scogan develops in even greater detail a "Rational State" that anticipates the systematic conditioning and caste separation of *Brave New World*. Tempting as it is, it would be wrong, however, to jump to the conclusion that the later novel is merely an amplification of the earlier. There are simply too many additions and shifts of emphasis—the Savage, Shakespeare, the Reservation, Ford and consumerism, for example—for that to be true. But there still remains enough connection, especially in the area of the scientific control of human physical and mental development, to give pause for thought.

Could Joseph Needham therefore be right in maintaining that Huxley borrowed heavily from Bertrand Russell's *The Scientific Outlook*, a judgment later echoed by H. V. Routh's *English Literature and Ideas in the Twentieth Century* (1946) and expanded by Philip Thody in his recent study of Huxley to the point where "one wonders at times if Huxley put any original ideas into his book"?[5] Russell's *Scientific Outlook* was first published in 1931, ten years after *Crome Yellow*. Is it true, as Ronald Clark suggests a good deal less polemically, that Huxley owes some sort of debt to J. B. S. Haldane's *Daedalus or Science and the Future*?[6] Haldane's book was first published in 1923, two years after *Crome Yellow*. On the face of it and judging only by the dates of publication, it looks very much as if the situation were reversed, as if Russell and Haldane were the borrowers, not Huxley.

The dates, however, are deceptive, for Huxley had known both of these men years before he began to write *Crome Yellow*. He had met Russell frequently at Garsington in the late stages of the war, and he had actually lived in Haldane's parental home, Cherwell, during his first year at Oxford. Until Huxley began inserting them into his books, not always in the most amiable way, Russell and

Haldane probably considered him a friend. Just as important, both men were in close touch with Julian Huxley at a time when the latter was carrying out original research of his own in genetics. And Julian Huxley certainly needs to be considered an extremely important intermediary on scientific matters for his brother, and perhaps even an original source, despite his disclaimer in the *Memorial Volume* that his brother ever came to him "for help over the biological facts and ideas he utilised so brilliantly in *Brave New World* and elsewhere."[7]

Russell seems in some respects the most logical possibility, especially if Eliot was right in identifying him with Scogan. Why choose Russell unless he was in some way associated with these ideas? And so he may have been, since Russell was a brilliant thinker and conversationalist on a wide variety of unconventional subjects. But no tangible proof exists, so far as I have been able to determine, showing that Russell was thinking specifically along Scogan's lines before 1924. In that year he published *Icarus*, a reply to and, in some ways, a refutation of Haldane's *Daedalus*.[8] The priority here, however, belongs clearly to Haldane; it was he who had raised the issue and Russell who had chimed in. Russell's interest in the subject is revealed by the fact that he *did* bother to write this kind of book, but that again is no proof of that interest's predating *Crome Yellow*. Occasional resemblances, such as his preference for an unjust society with a "higher" purpose to a happy one without, as at the close of *Roads to Freedom* (1918), are of so general a nature as hardly to matter.

With Haldane, the situation is rather different. Although *Daedalus* itself did not appear until after *Crome Yellow*, the substance of its argument goes back as far as 1912, when Haldane was still an undergraduate at Oxford and shortly before Huxley came to live at Cherwell. Nine years later, at just about the time Huxley was getting down to work on *Crome Yellow*, Haldane refurbished his essay and read it before the New College Essay Society.[9] Haldane's friend and later collaborator, Julian Huxley, was also at Oxford at this time as a biology don and if not actually present at this meeting may be assumed to have heard about it from Haldane. The chances are extremely good that Aldous Huxley knew about the essentials of what was to become *Daedalus* by 1921 at the latest. That he did know the book in its finished form is absolutely çertain from a reference to it in *Proper Studies* (277). Interestingly enough, both of the relevant passages in *Proper Studies* and *Crome Yellow* mention a supposed "experiment" by Erasmus Darwin and Anna Seward ("The Swan of Lichfield") in trying to grow a human embryo artificially. There is, perhaps understandably, no mention of such an experiment in any of the literature about either Darwin or Seward, and the story bears all the earmarks of a Haldane anecdote.

From Haldane, Huxley seems to have borrowed several important features of his future state. There is, to begin with, an analogous emphasis on stability, with Haldane predicting that the important transition will be from the old stable agricultural society to the new industrial one. The people who first make that transition will, according to Haldane, inherit the earth. This is, of course, precisely what has happened in Huxley's novel: the newest of stable industrial societies matched, in the Pueblo, by the oldest of stable agricultural ones. Second, Haldane discusses a historical instance of raising industrial productivity by chemical means and goes on to envision the development of a wide variety of new and pleasurable stimulants; this might have been the hint Huxley needed to produce the "warm liquor" of *Crome Yellow* that was eventually to ferment into *soma*. But more important than either of these is the "Extracts from an Essay on the Influence of Biology on History during the Twentieth Century" written by an undergraduate a hundred and fifty years in the future. Here Haldane proposes the technique of reproduction that he calls ectogenesis but that has become popularly known a "test-tube babies." Significantly, the "Extracts" begins at precisely the point where *Brave New World* does: at the "hatchery"; and significantly Haldane goes on to predict that the "abolition of disease will make death a physiological event like sleep." The outlines of the new world's birth and death control, it is evident, already exist in *Daedalus*.[10]

Haldane may also have exercised a more indirect influence on *Brave New World*. In 1926 his wife, Charlotte Haldane, published an anti-utopian novel, *Man's World*, which in some ways is very much like Huxley's novel. (That Haldane is the source of the scientific background of his wife's story is certain, since her desire for his advice led to their first meeting). In *Man's World* there is a kind of prototype of a World Controller, Mensch, who founds a world state by enlisting the impressionable young and by training them to take over command. In this new society, old age is abolished and each generation lives and dies together; there is a separate class of women who have been found eugenically fit to be mothers; and, most important of all, there are no more individuals. The plot of *Man's World* resembles that of Huxley's novel by tracing the increasingly conscious resistance of one man against the "happy" norm, a resistance that culminates, like the Savage's, in suicide. By an appropriate sequence of events, when *Brave New World* was published, Charlotte Haldane was selected to review it for *Nature*. Her verdict was that it was "a very great book," second only to *Antic Hay*, but she made no mention of its relation either to her own work or to that of her husband.[11]

Both Russell's *Icarus* and *The Scientific Outlook* are links in the chain first forged by Haldane, but they also go well beyond their original. The choice of Icarus, for example, clearly suggests a rather less hearty confidence in the future of science than Haldane's Daedalus. Hence Russell's focus is, like Huxley's, more on the effects of scientific advances on man than on machinery. He foresees, among other possibilities, the development of advertising and propaganda as weapons to suppress freedom, as well as social destiny control by genetic means. "Against the injections of the State Physicians," Russell argues in a passage that evokes the Savage's haranguing of the Delta workers, "the most eloquent socialist oratory would be powerless."[12] *The Scientific Outlook* goes even beyond this in its suspicion of the promises of science, foreseeing as it does the elimination of "all that is tragic in human life" and the discovery of the chemical means to prevent man from ever being unhappy. Dangerous writers of the past, such as Shakespeare, would only be accessible to special students by government license. Along with the biochemical means of destiny control already broached in *Icarus*, there would also be a biochemical "mood control," which would supplement regular doses of Hollywood-like entertainment. In Russell's future there would be no equality, but a strict intellectual hierarchy, with black laborers occupying the bottom rungs. On the higher levels especially, "all private sentiments would be viewed with suspicion"; and all nonreconditionable deviants would be consigned to the lethal chamber.[13]

The resemblances to *Brave New World* are striking, but they are perhaps less so if one grants that they are in nearly every case anticipated by *Crome Yellow*. Moreover, *The Scientific Outlook* and *Brave New World*, one should remember, were published within a few months of each other, so that it seems unlikely that Huxley could have had sufficient time even to read it. And besides, the differences are just as striking as the resemblances. Russell's governing elite, with its Spartan stress on hardship and endurance—rolling in the snow, for example—is closer to an English public school or to Wells's *samurai* than to anything in *Brave New World*. The same is true of his view that the destructive urges of future man will be channeled into sadistic experiments of a quasi-religious nature, which will claim their "holocausts of sacred victims." Russell considers this cruelty a "ray of hope" since it is the weak spot that may cause the whole structure to collapse.[14] But in *Brave New World*, with its Violent Passion Surrogates, that eventuality does not even arise.

That Russell exercised some influence on Huxley's novel seems likely, though it was probably more in conversation than through his writings.[15] However, Russell was by no means, as we have seen in the case of Haldane, above being influenced himself. For that matter, Scogan-Russell's separation of his future state into the categories of men of reason, men of faith, and the herd, comes straight from Gustave LeBon's widely read *The Crowd* (1895; English trans. 1896); even the example of Luther as an archetypal man of faith is LeBon's.[16]

Be this as it may, it is more important to ask why three highly gifted men came to share a preoccupation about the dangers of science at just this juncture than to try to allot just the right amount of credit where it is due. In a sense, the answer to this larger question is easy: it was because developments in science, especially in genetics and psychology, had reached a stage where this sort of response became possible. But while this is true, it is by no means the whole story. Without trying to tell that whole story, it needs to be said that *Brave New World*, along with Haldane and Russell's books of popularized science, are products of the resurgence of the materialist-idealist schism in the sciences (and in philosophy) at the opening of the century, a schism due chiefly to the general acceptance of Einstein's theory of relativity. "Einstein has told us," Haldane wrote in *Daedalus*, "that space, time, and matter are shadows of the fifth dimension, and the heavens have declared his glory. In consequence Kantian idealism will become the basal working hypothesis of the physicist and finally of all educated men, just as materialism did after Newton's day."[17] The same point is made at greater length in A. N. Whitehead's extremely influential *Science in the Modern World* and in E. A. Burtt's *Metaphysical Foundations of Modern Science*, which for time became a kind of handbook for Huxley.

By the teens and twenties the controversy began to spill over into biology and psychology, in part because of the growing impact of Bergsonian philosophy. Again the age-old battle was joined: was man matter or was he idea, or was he a mixture of both? Outright or absolute idealists were rarities, but there were many modified idealists or "vitalists"—including Huxley, Haldane, and Russell—and even more materialists or "mechanists." (The vitalists were also sometimes called "finalists," since they frequently posited a purpose for life. Some of the terminology and a good deal of the matter of this controversy goes back at least as far as La Mettrie's *L'Homme machine*.)[18]

In biology, the conflict was particularly acute in genetics, which seemed on the verge of explaining the origins of life and even beginning to think of creating it. It was this area which was the particular province of J. B. S. Haldane and Julian Huxley, both of whom adopted the vitalist position that life could not be explained by the mechanical analogy alone. In the opposing camp were figures like Lancelot Hogben, who argued in *The Nature of Living Matter* (1930) that such progress as had been made in genetics hitherto "has at every stage involved the elimination of holistic concepts by the ruthless application of mechanistic logic."[19]

The real battleground, however, and the one that received most public attention, was psychology. The experiments by Pavlov on the conditioned reflexes of dogs suggested that so-called voluntary behavior was—or at least could be made into—merely another form of conditioned behavior. As Hogben observed, this new school of psychologists followed "the express object of making psychology a physical science, relieving man, the celestial pilgrim, of the burden of his soul."[20] Pavlov's American disciple, J. B. Watson, carried this method of research over into the study of man. "Give me a dozen healthy infants, well-formed," he proclaimed in *Behaviorism* (1919), "and my own specified world to bring them up in and I'll guarantee to take any one at random and train him to become any type of specialist I might select—doctor, lawyer, artist, merchant-chief and, yes, even beggar-man and thief, regardless of his talents, penchants, tendencies, abilities, vocations, and race of his ancestors."[21] In a later and even more polemical contribution to *The Battle of Behaviorism* (1928), Watson attacked the vitalistic point of view by name. "*The behaviorist finds no scientific evidence,*" he wrote in emphatic italics, "*for the existence of any vitalistic principle,* such, for example, as Mr. McDougall's 'purpose.' . . . We need nothing to explain behavior but the ordinary laws of physics and chemistry."[22] William McDougall, Watson's opponent and the other contributor to the *Battle,* is one of the few modern psychologists whom Huxley consistently mentions with favor in his letters and elsewhere.

For Huxley, the mechanists and Watson in particular were bugbears. *Brave New World* is chiefly an attack on the mechanization of life, an attempt to demolish the robot utopia of Wellsian "little fat men," as Orwell saw at once.[23] The opening scene of chapter 2, in which a group of infants is conditioned by means of sirens and alarm bells (plus a mild electric shock), is closely modeled on one of Watson's best-known neo-Pavlovian experiments.[24] The choice of the surname Watson for one of the more important characters of the novel again indicates the relation between mechanism and the new world. For that matter, the names Foster, Bernard, and Helmholtz, which also feature prominently in the novel, allude to three of the greatest physiologists of the nineteenth century: Sir Michael Foster (1836–1907), a former assistant of T. H. Huxley's who succeeded him at the Royal Institution and who wrote, among other well-known biological works, *The Elements of Embryology* (1874); Claude Bernard (1813–1878), the greatest of French physiologists, credited with first putting medicine on a scientific footing; and Hermann von Helmholtz (1821–1894), the German physiologist who is best known as the formulator of the law of the conservation of energy. In the new world, genetics and psychology are intimately linked, housed as they are together in the District Hatchery and Conditioning Centers. Mechanistic physiology and mechanistic psychology, not surprisingly, produce mechanical man.

What does seem surprising, however, is the introduction into this context of Freudian psychology. Our Freud, as the World Controller remarks, is the name which Our Ford for inscrutable reasons used when he spoke out on psychological matters. As Huxley knew very well, mechanistic psychologists like Watson were adamantly opposed to Freud; for them, consciousness was the last refuge of the soul. But why then bring in Freud? One answer might be that Huxley despised the Freudians as much as he did the behaviorists, which is probably true but still does not explain how the differences between these two schools are reconciled in the new world. Since Our Freud does not really speak out much—certainly a great deal less than Our Ford—his function may either be purely decorative (a contemporary allusion that even the dullest of Huxley's readers would be sure to grasp) or else, as Philip Thody argues, to symbolize the attitude that any kind of repression of one's impulses, especially sexual ones, is wrong.[25] Thody's explanation is, I think, correct as far as it goes. He overlooks, however, the related point that Huxley is seeking to make through Freud, namely to trace the consequences (as Huxley wrote to his father, of all people) "of the abolition fo the family and all the Freudian 'complexes' for which family relationships are responsible" (L, 351). It is Freud, not Watson, who is ultimately responsible for the Hatchery and Conditioning Centre. Freud provides the rationale, the Behaviorists only the staff. He is the closest the new world's science comes to having a conscience.

The relevant texts belong to Freud's late period, notably *The Future of an Illusion* (1927; English trans. 1928) and *Civilization and its Discontents* (1930, German and English). Both of these essays relate in significant ways to the mechanist-vitalist controversy and to *Brave New World*."One would think," Freud writes in the opening pages of the earlier essay, "that a re-ordering of human relationships should be possible, which would remove the sources of dissatisfaction with civilization by renouncing coercion and the suppression of the instincts, so that, undisturbed by internal discord, men might devote themselves to the acquisition of wealth and its enjoyment. That would be the golden age, but it is questionable if such a state of affairs can be realized." Questionable? In *Brave New World* there is no more question about it; here we have the conflictless, nonsuppressive consumer society in full flower. Furthermore, the atheistic Freud goes on to argue, the great mistakes in modern education are "the retardation of sexual development and premature religious influence," mistakes for which the only real cure is large doses of scientific knowledge. The religious illusion has no future, but as for science, "no, our science is no illusion."[26] To it therefore belongs the future.

Civilization and Its Discontents consists largely of a more extensive reexamination of the same issues. Here again God and finalism are dispatched in short order. For Freud "the idea of life having a purpose stands and falls with the religious system," and since the latter falls, so does the former. Freud therefore concerns himself with the "less ambitious question of what men themselves show by their behavior to be the purpose and intention of their lives." The answer to this is immediately apparent: "they strive after happiness; they want to become happy and remain so." But achieving positive happiness seems impossible in the universe as presently arranged; the best man can hope for is to avoid unhappiness. Of the various means of realizing this end, "the most interesting . . . are those which seek to influence our own organism [i.e., by chemical means]. In the last analysis, all suffering is nothing else than sensation; it only exists insofar as we feel it, and we only feel it in consequence of certain ways in which our organism is regulated."[27]

Here Freud comes very close to the mechanist position of someone like Watson and even closer to the position of Mustapha Mond in *Brave New World*. Mond also rejects the notion that life might have a meaning beyond itself. The paper on "A New Theory of Biology," which he reads and admires, must be rejected because of its vitalist assumptions. Serious science, like serious art, as he later points out to the Savage and his friends, is incompatible with happiness and must therefore be kept within limits prescribed by a "cookery book, with an orthodox theory of cooking which nobody's allowed to question" (185); this cookbook produces food for the belly but not for the mind—technology, not science. In the ensuing theological discussion, during which Mond reads to the Savage excerpts from Newman and Maine de Biran, the same point is made again: "God isn't compatible with machinery and scientific medicine and universal happines. You must make your choice. Our civilisation has chosen machinery and medicine and happiness" (192). In this retelling of Dostoevski's parable, the Grand Inquisitor is a mechanist and Christ a vitalist.

Freud, to be sure, is aware that civilization as we know it in the twentieth century rests on a foundation of discontent. That, as the title of his essay suggests, is the crux of the issue—whether the conflict between individual liberty and corporate conformity can be resolved or whether civilization must always have its discontents. It is the sublimation of instinct rather than its satisfaction that makes for cultural development; it is restraint that "makes it possible for higher psychical activities, scientific, artistic or ideological, to play such an important part in civilized life."[28] In the Fordian society, the individual is no longer free to endanger himself or his group by refusing to indulge his impulses. Resistance on the part of a few individuals of the first Fordian commandment is, in fact, what makes up the plot of *Brave New World*. Most obviously, the Savage exercises self-restraint; he realizes that without restraint there is lust but never love; hence his apparently absurd behavior toward Lenina. When he fails to restrain himself, as in the orgy at the end of the novel, he ceases to be "civilized" (on his own terms), and therefore kills himself.

The Savage's fate is probably to be read as the inevitable consequence of behavior conditioned by a society quite as rigid as the Fordian one, only in a reverse direction. The same is true, however, neither of Bernard Marx nor of Helmholtz Watson, the two other nonconformists. Bernard's experience parallels that of the Savage, though without any of the Savage's intensity of feeling. He shocks the pneumatic Lenina by regretting the speed with which they went to bed for the first time. "He began to talk a lot of incomprehensible and dangerous nonsense. Lenina did her best to stop the ears of her mind; but every now and then a phrase would insist on becoming audible. ' . . . to try the effect of arresting my impulses,' she heard him say . . . 'I want to know what passion is . . . I want to feel something strongly,'" (77). So too with Helmholtz Watson, who abandons his women and his committees for the sake of examining the effects of abstinence. "A physical shortcoming could produce a kind of mental excess. The process, it seemed, was reversible. Mental excess could produce, for its own purposes, the voluntary blindness and deafness of deliberate solitude, the artificial impotence of asceticism" (57). It is this process that also leads to his shockingly anti-social poem about solitude and to his eventual exile to the Falkland Islands.

Paradoxically, Marx and Watson have strictly adhered to Freud's precept to supersede "infantilism," though Freud intended his injunction to be interpreted rather differently in *The Future of an Illusion*.[29] Both have deliberately attempted to set up obstacles for themselves that will impede the easy realization of their desires. In doing so, they have also demonstrated Huxley's dictum that what he called moral flat racing, the characteristically modern morality, is boring. "No reasonable hedonist," Huxley wrote in "Obstacle Race" (1931), "can consent to be a flat racer. Abolishing obstacles, he abolishes half his pleasure. And at the same time he abolishes most of his dignity as a human being. For the dignity of man consists precisely in his ability to restrain himself from dashing away along the flat, in his capacity to raise obstacles in his own path."[30] A "genuinely scientific future state" would therefore, in Huxley's view, create unnatural obstacles to heighten pleasure and to create at least a semblance of human dignity. The Fordian state is in this sense not genuinely scientific, for it has no real conscience. It can tolerate sensation but never feeling, and feeling, as Mustapha Mond says, lurks in that interval of time between desire and its consummation"(45). In Ford's world the race must be unutterably flat, it must never end, it must lead nowhere, and it must be closed to all drivers above an emotional age of five.

Huxley was well acquainted with Freud's work and had mocked it as far back as his student days at Oxford, in the short story "Eupompus Gave Splendour to Art by Numbers" (1916), and a little later in "The Farcical History of Richard Greenow." In the character of Mary Bracegirdle in *Crome Yellow* Huxley again gave vent to his contempt for a pseudo-science that only served to mislead simple-minded people. Essays like "Our Contemporary Hocus Pocus" (1925), "A Case of Voluntary Ignorance" (1956), and "The Oddest Science" (1957) testify by their very titles to Huxley's lifelong interest in and suspicion of psychoanalysis of the Freudian variety. For Jung, on the other hand, he felt great admiration, at any rate in the 1920s. In the Introduction to *Proper Studies* (1927), he praises Jung as "by far the most gifted" of the psychoanalysts, but also gives high marks to Cardinal Newman, "whose analysis of the psychology of thought remains one of the most acute, as it is certainly the most elegant, ever made." For the rest, however, modern psychoanalysts are "either uninspired, unilluminating, and soundly dull, or else, like Freud and Adler, mono-maniacal" (xix). In *Jesting Pilate* he blames materialism generally and Freud specifically for doing away with religion and creating a moral vacuum: "The moral conscience was abolished (another illusion) and 'amuse yourself' proclaimed as the sole categorical imperative. The theories of Freud were received in intellectual circles with acclaim; to explain every higher activity of the human mind in terms of incest and coprophilia came to be regarded not only as truly scientific, but also as somehow virile and courageous. Freudism became the *realpolitik* of psychology and philosophy" (275). In the *Letters*, too, he either makes fun of Freudian analysis or else attacks it as pernicious and harmful, as, for example, when criticizing Middleton Murry's *Son of Woman: The Story of D. H. Lawrence* (1931) for "exploiting . . . the psycho-analytical rigmarole, which will fetch 100's of earnest imbeciles" (L, 355).[31]

Huxley was by no means alone in his contempt for Freud and Freud's followers. A. Wohlgemuth's *A Critical Examination of Psycho-Analysis* (1923) systematically demolishes Freud's theories, as does Abraham Myerson's "Freud's Theory of Sex: A Criticism" (1929). The chances are good that Huxley knew at least the latter work, since it forms part of W. F. Calverton and S. D. Schmalhausen's *Sex in Civilization* (1929), a book that also contains extracts from two letters by Huxley to Schmalhausen. Of these, more in a moment.

Schmalhausen was also the author of *Why We Misbehave* (1928), which Huxley had definitely read. In this book, especially in the chapter entitled "The Freudian Emphasis on Sex," Schmalhausen sets out to show how "the contemporary cultural situation is subordinating procreation to recreation." Basically in sympathy with Freud at this stage, Schmalhausen agrees that "civilization spells repression," or at any rate what Schmalhausen calls "conventional civilization" leads to repression. But he voices the hope that "perhaps men and women can build a new civilization which will not rest upon the props of repression and concealment." This future "new civilization" is already being realized through the "New Morality," which is "really new in the original sense that it assigns a status of reasonable respectability to behavior branded throughout the moralistic Christian countries as immoral, disreputable: for example, auto-eroticism, adultery, easy divorce, promiscuity, homosexual affection, casualness in love life."[32] The tones that are being sounded here might almost be those of an early twentieth-century Mustapha Mond.

Similar tones—similarly inspired, at least in part, by Freud and the "new morality"—were also being sounded closer to home, by Bertrand Russell and by his then wife, Dora. In *The Right to Be Happy* (1927), Dora Russell launches a direct attack against the old Christian morality and pleads for the guiltless enjoyment of sex, by men and, especially, by women. There must be no more sin and there must be no more special and subsidiary role for women. Motherhood in particular must be removed from sexuality, for "very few have yet understood that the real problem of feminism is the emancipation of mothers." A new sense of the family is developing because, "under the influence of Freudian theories, modern people are rapidly casting aside their asceticism about sexual desires, but they are developing asceticism about parenthood. They renounce any close relationship with their children because they regard this as necessarily sexual, and likely to lead to dangerous neuroses in the children as well as themselves." Motherhood, if not fatherhood, is here already on the way to becoming a dirty word. Moreover, it is because modern civilization refuses to recognize and to allow outlets for "instinct and the anarchic impulses of human nature" that this civilization is doomed to fail and, presumably, to be replaced by one that will provide such outlets. Religion is especially pernicious and so Dora Russell singles out Aldous Huxley for "maintaining that religions . . . are expressions of the Life Force."[33]

Bertrand Russell's *Marriage and Morals* (1929) is a more sophisticated version of his wife's book. Here Russell also foresees a decline in the importance of the family, partly because the state will take and already is taking over the role of the father. Fathers will soon be abolished, at least for any function beyond impregnation. Indeed, in the scientifically planned future state, two or three percent of the males and about twenty-five percent of the females will be set aside for the "purpose of propagation. There will be, presumably at puberty, an examination, as a result of which all unsuccessful candidates will be sterilized. The father will have no more connection with his offspring than a bull or stallion has at present, and the mother will be a specialized professional, distinguished from other women by her manner of life. I do not say that this state of affairs is going to come about, still less do I say that I desire it, for I confess that I find it exceedingly repugnant. Nevertheless, when the matter is examined objectively, it is seen that such a plan might produce remarkable results." These remarkable results, with modifications such as the complete *in vitro* gestation of the fetus, have been fully realized in *Brave New World,* as has the entire divorce between sexuality and parenthood also predicted by Russell.[34] In this way, as Russell notes in another book, *The Conquest of Happiness* (1930), "victims of maternal 'virtue'" will be liberated "from the tyranny of early beliefs and affections" and will therefore be able to make "the first step towards happiness."[35]

How "happy" the early practitioners of this new morality actually were may be doubted. According to one observer, Douglas Goldring, their happiness was indistinguishable from unhappiness. Although, as he writes in *Odd Man Out* (1935), "the works of Dr. Marie Stopes and other birth controllers and sexologists were eagerly studied, together with those of Dr. Freud, at the women's colleges in Oxford and Cambridge, at the London School of Economics, and at other progressive educational centres throughout England," the results of such study were meager in terms of real happiness. For the consequence was that "the boys and girls of the middle classes, particularly the 'intellectuals,' may be said, like the Scotsman, to have 'fornicated gravely but without conviction.'"[36]

In the novels and stories of the twenties, Huxley had examined the progress and effects of the new morality and had found these to be sorely disappointing. Though he was fond of entertaining odd and even shocking social and religious hypotheses, and considered himself on occasion to be a pyrrhonist, Huxley was and remained fundamentally a moralist—even a moralist of the old Swiftian school. For him, in the final analysis, the moral world was neither chaotic nor relative. "Values," as he put it at the close of *Jesting Pilate,* "are everywhere and in all kinds of society broadly the same," and the duty of the world traveler—or, for that matter, of the pilgrim in progress—was to "distinguish between harmless perversions and those which tend to deny or stultify the fundamen-

tal values. Towards the first he will be tolerant. There can be no
compromise with the second" (290–91). In *Brave New World* there
is no such compromise.

In the two letters to Schmalhausen referred to earlier, Huxley
provides a summary of his objections to the new sexual morality
and, implicitly, to the sexual ethic of the new world state. Both of
these letters appear to date from 1928 and, because of their intrinsic interest, as well as the fact that their existence has not been
known to readers of Huxley, they are worth quoting from fairly
extensively. In the first letter Huxley expresses his doubt as to
"whether the kind of cold promiscuity current in youthful circles
today is much more satisfactory than the restraints it has replaced.
It is as much an expression of the consciousness's hatred for instinct
and the body as was puritanism—puritanism inside out. A more
fundamental change involving an alteration in our evaluation of
consciousness (at present too high) is required." This statement
could almost have been written by D. H. Lawrence, but the second letter is more authentic Huxley: "My own feeling about the
present sexual license is that recreative love [Schmalhausen's term
for sexual promiscuity] is apt to be as killing to passion as the most
repressive puritanism; in a sense more so, as passion is the product
of sexual impulse and some inward repression. When the repression is removed, the impulse wastes itself emptily. I have developed this in an article which will appear in the next few months
in Vanity Fair [probably "The Cold Blooded Romantics," March
1928], suggesting that the restraint now acceptable is the restraint
arising from a mythology of Personality, in which the myth of
Personality-as-a-whole takes the place of the now incredible myth
of an absolute god or good. That is to say the interests or part of the
personality are to be restrained in those of the whole. But in any
case the essential thing is restraint, without which, it seems to me,
there can be no passion or love, only a cold lasciviousness."[37]

Restraint is the defining characteristic of the fully human individual; only by means of restraint can one gain access to those
states of being, like passion or love, which are traditionally recognized as the highest states possible to mortal existence. It is restraint, and the overcoming of restraint, that allows Romeo to love
Juliet rather than merely make love to her; it is self-restraint that
keeps Prospero from ever falling to the level of Caliban. It is also

restraint, voluntary restraint, that, as Huxley well knew and as the Savage exemplifies, can lead beyond passion and love to a kind of divine ecstasy. This is what William James had pointed out in *Varieties of Religious Experience* (1902), a work which Huxley valued highly and which might be said to stand at exactly the opposite pole to Freud's *The Future of an Illusion*. In *Brave New World* excessive restraint, like the Savage's, still leads to self-destruction; but as Huxley grew farther and farther away from Lawrence's ethic of total personality, he came to see that not only the truth in life but also the truth beyond life lay in restraint, the restraint of the great mystics and not merely the restraint of the great lovers and tragic heroes.[38]

"Whether we like it or not," Huxley remarked in *Literature and Science,* his last completed work, "ours is the Age of Science." Whether we like it or not, and Huxley had come to like it less and less as the Age of Science revealed itself more and more, in gas chambers and in atom bombs and in the abrogation of individual liberty. He denounced our age for worshiping the golden calf of mass production and for imposing as the whole truth the most systematic body of half-truths ever assembled. Something needed to be done, it was clear, but the question was what? "What can a writer do about it?" he asked. "And what, as a conscientious literary artist and a responsible citizen, ought he to do about it?"(60). His duty, the answer came, was to render as truthfully and perfectly as he could those private and individual worlds—quite as real as the public ones—which were forever closed off to science; to make the best of the world as it is; to give form to everyday life; to allow us to know who we are. Bad art, Huxley warned, was just as dangerous as bad religion or bad philosophy; it was a crime against society.

Has *Brave New World,* judged by these criteria, done its duty? No, one must—perhaps a little surprisingly—admit, it has not. There are practically no individuals in the novel; there is little life as we know it; and there is almost no opportunity to come to a knowledge of ourselves. Should we conclude, then, that Huxley has failed? No, quite as certainly not, for precisely the reason that he has not shown us ourselves—but only the selves that we have not yet come to be. For with a power seldom equaled in the literature of the Age of Science, Huxley has exhorted us to make

the humanly best of what we still have and are—a society of dispa-
rate, dissident, and unhappy individuals—lest we be overtaken by
a future in which responsible citizens and artists (and we) no longer
exist.

3

From Savages to Men Like Gods

It is communism based, not on poverty but on riches, not on humility but on pride, not on sacrifice but on complete fulfilment in the flesh of all strong desire, not in Heaven but in earth. We will be Sons of God who walk here on earth, not bent on getting and having, because we know we inherit all things. We will be aristocrats, and as wise as the serpent in dealing with the mob. For the mob shall not crush us nor starve us nor cry us to death. We will deal cunningly with the mob, the greedy soul, we will gradually bring it to subjection.

From the *Letters* of D. H. Lawrence

The European talks of progress because by the aid of a few scientific discoveries he has established a society which has mistaken comfort for civilization.

Benjamin Disraeli

H. G. Wells's future has finally caught up with him and, by an irony that he would have been among the first to appreciate, it has forgotten him. Not altogether selflessly, but with an astonishing literary energy and determination he toiled half a century, drawing up blueprints of a future filled with gadgets and—to use Orwell's phrase—enlightened sunbathers. What a pity that he did not live to see the Costa Brava swarming with tanned nudity and transitor radio sets. For a whole generation of readers growing up between 1900 and 1930, this little, fat, and jolly man, half prophet and half huckster, became identified with the shape of things to come. The very mention of the future, J. B. S. Haldane noted in 1924, necessarily evoked his name. Only Jules Verne rivaled him as a writer of

57

scientific romances, and Verne's future was already fading into reality by the time Wells reached the peak of his popular success in the early twenties.

Not surprisingly, therefore, Wells was a favorite target for those who did not share his confidence in the future or in science. As Mark Hillegas has suggested in his interesting study of Wells's literary enemies, *The Future as Nightmare*, to be against utopia and to be against Wells were, during the first half of this century, very nearly synonymous. To this rule Aldous Huxley was no exception. Nor did Huxley take any special pains to hide the fact that in *Brave New World* he was, among other things, blasting Wells. On the contrary, Wells is one of only two contemporary writers to be mentioned by name in the novel—thinly disguised as "Dr. Wells"—the other being Shaw. In at least one letter dating from the period during which he was working on the novel, Huxley openly avowed his aim to expose the "horror of the Wellsian Utopia", (L. 348) and some thirty years later he even named Wells's *Men Like Gods* (1923) as the inspiration for a parody that later "got out of hand and turned into something quite different from what I intended."[1]

Somewhere behind Our Ford and Our Freud, then, lurks Our Wells. He bears rather the same relation to *Brave New World* that Leibniz does to *Candide*, for—rightly or wrongly—Huxley identified Wells, as he wrote in a letter to T. S. Eliot, with "Wellsian Progress" (L. 380), with the doctrine that man can live by technology alone and with the presumption that men could come to be like unto gods. Wells, in Huxley's view, had merely shifted the tense of Pangloss's best-of-all-possible-worlds from the present into the future. For the skeptical Huxley, as for the skeptical Voltaire, the real world was a fallen one.

Ironically, the apple that Wells proffered modern man was a Huxleyan growth. Before becoming a novelist and a Fabian socialist, Wells had been a biologist, trained for a brief time by the great T. H. Huxley himself. Wells had imbibed natural selection at the fountainhead, but natural selection, as Darwin's bulldog knew, had at least left Nature red in tooth and claw in place of the vanished divinity, whereas artificial selection, in the form now proposed by Wells, left only man. Perhaps this is why Wells appears in *Brave New World* as a doctor, rather than in any other guise. What the grandfather had given, the grandson now hoped to take away. Poetic, or at least novelistic, justice would be done.

Wells was deeply offended by *Brave New World,* interpreting the attack personally and blustering about Huxley's "betrayal" of the future. Even as late as 1940, it still rankled sufficiently for him to go out of his way, in *The New World Order,* to denounce that "Bible of the impotent genteel, Huxley's *Brave New World;*" and in the same year he told Klaus Mann that he thought Huxley was a "fool." Wells believed that he had been misrepresented by this "disagreeable fantasy."[2] His resentment, one must in all fairness admit, was not altogether unjustified. Anyone who has the stamina to read through the mass of Wells's scientific fantasies will soon discover that he was not always a facile optimist, especially in his earlier books. In *The Time Machine* (1895), for instance, one of the best known of them all, he draws a remarkable portrait of man's eventual degeneration and extinction. Nor was the early Wells unaware of the dangers of science. The pursuit of scientific knowledge for its own sake and without reference to a system of moral values leads to disaster in *The Island of Dr. Moreau* (1896) and in *The Invisible Man* (1897). And in two other, related works, "The Story of Days to Come" (1899) and *When the Sleeper Wakes* (1899), he demonstrates in detail how worlds controlled by technical ingenuity and moral ineptitude can go dangerously awry. Even in *Men Like Gods* and *A Modern Utopia* (1905), Wells warns against states which, no matter how ideal in other respects, prefer uniformity to individuality. As his own unconventional life amply testifies, he was all for individual freedom. "I am neither a pessimist nor an optimist at bottom," he declared in 1934, and one is rather tempted to agree with that verdict.[3]

But to yield wholly to this temptation would be wrong. The early Wells is quite a different creature from the middle Wells, and even the warnings of the early period are more warnings against capitalist science than against science as such. Until the last two years of his life when he took it all back and asked for an epitaph reading "God damn you all: I told you so,"[4] Wells had always been enough of a socialist and meliorist to believe that democracy, reason, and science would in the long run triumph over selfishness and willful ignorance. Like a kind of socialist Christ, the Sleeper at the end of *When the Sleeper Wakes* takes upon himself the injustices of this world and, sacrificing his own life, destroys the forces of oligarchy and ushers in the age of scientific socialism. The relish with which Wells contemplates the coming of this secular paradise is perhaps best conveyed by the conclusion of "A Story of the Days to Come," where a dying oligarch goes to seek help from a young doctor. "Why should we save you in particular?" the doctor asks. "You see—from one point of view—people with imaginations and passions like yours have to go—they have to go."

"Go?"
"Die out. It's an eddy."
He was a young man with a serene face. He smiled at Bindon. "We get on with research, you know; we give advice when people have the sense to ask for it. And we bide our time."
"Bide your time?"
"We hardly know enough yet to take over the management, you know."
"You needn't be anxious. Science is young yet. It's got to keep on growing for a few generations. . . . Some day—some day, men will live in a different way." He looked at Bindon and meditated. "There'll be a lot of dying out before that day can come."[5]

When this sort of doctor finally succeeds, he becomes, one suspects, either a ranking member of the scientific-socialistic samurai of *A Modern Utopia*, or else a Fordian Dr. Wells. Or worse.

What Huxley questioned in Wells's future worlds was not the good intentions, but the bad conclusions. Was it really possible for all men to be equal, as Wells and the socialists seemed to maintain? If, by means of genetic control and artificial selection, as in *Men Like Gods*, "every individual is capable of playing the superior part, who will consent," Huxley asked in *Proper Studies*, "or be content to do the dirty work and obey? The inhabitants of Mr. Wells's numerous utopias solve the problem by ruling and being ruled, doing high-brow and low-brow work, in turns . . . an admirable state of affairs if it could be arranged . . . though personally, I find my faith too weak." If men could be bred into gods, Huxley argued, they would also quarrel like gods, with a consequent and ineluctable *Götterdämmerung*. All order is hierarchical order. Cut the great chain of being and you cut yourself adrift. "States function as smoothly as they do," Huxley concludes, "because the greater part of the population is not very intelligent, dreads responsibility, and desires nothing better than to be told what to do. . . . A state with a population consisting of nothing but these superior people could not hope to last for a year" (281–82).

The dream of universal equality is, in Huxley's view, just that: a dream. When you try to put the dream into practice, you get—what? A nightmare. This, in sum, is the meaning of the so-called Cyprus Experiment in *Brave New World*, in which a population of twenty-two thousand Alpha-plus men and women are given the run of the island and complete control over their own destinies. Within twenty years—after massive infighting—the three thousand survivors petition to be readmitted into the Fordian world.

Huxley's chief objections, then, to Wells are that he is unrealistic, that his estimate of human nature is completely out of whack, and that his prophecies about the future are therefore dangerously misleading. Not that Wells alone is to be held responsible; he is merely the most visible exponent of a whole complex of attitudes, linking science with socialism and democracy. To some degree at least, Wells belongs to that class of old-style utopians whose conviction it was, as Huxley observed in 1931, that all one had to do was "get rid of priests and kings, make Aeschylus and the differential calculus available to all, and the world will become a paradise." But for Huxley democracy and universal education are not the philosopher's stone, turning lead into gold. Only science can perform this trick, and its price for doing so is prohibitive. Hence, Huxley argues—referring no doubt to himself and to the novel he was just then in the process of writing—"contemporary prophets have visions of future societies founded on the idea of natural inequality, not of natural equality . . . of a ruling aristocracy slowly improved . . . by deliberate eugenic breeding"; and further and even more directly pertinent to the hierarchical society of *Brave New World*, Huxley foresees the next generation's utopia being based on an intellectual caste system "accompanied by a Machiavellian system of education, designed to give the members of the lower castes only such education as it is profitable for society at large and the upper castes in particular that they should have" (*Music at Night*, 150–52).

To be sure, in both *Men Like Gods* and *A Modern Utopia*, there is an active program of eugenics, and in the latter there is even something of a caste separation between the "samurai" and the rest of the population, with further subdivisions within the samurai themselves. However, the samurai are a purely voluntary aristocracy, as are the more loosely organized "intelligences" who direct social and psychological affairs in *Men Like Gods*. A voluntary aristocracy on this scale, however, must have struck Huxley as an absurdity, as at best the equivalent of a voluntary bureaucracy, which is the function of the Alpha individuals in the Fordian world. To ensure stability, the ultimate control of a society must be vested in a very few hands, a condition which is true not merely of the stable Fordian state but also of the stable Pueblo Indian community.

The relation of *Brave New World* to Wells's fantasies is (with the exception of a number of technological details to be dealt with later) or a rather general nature. Though it may have started out as a parody of *Men Like Gods*, Huxley is quite right in insisting that *Brave New World* ended up as something quite different. It is no *Shamela* to Wells's *Pamela*. The only major areas at which the two novels intersect concern the emotions and the Savage. In Wells's utopia, as in Huxley's dystopia, deep feeling is either nonexistent or reprehensible. The explosion that kills three utopians and temporarily opens their world to Wells's mouthpiece, Barnstaple, and a few other less tractable earthlings occasions no grief among their fellows. Pity, in this utopia of pseudo-Nietzschean supermen, is a virtually unknown vice practiced furtively by degenerate throwbacks to primitive modern man. For the rest there is an athletic, no-nonsense attitude about the mental and emotional lives of these demi-gods that must have struck a responsive satirical cord in Huxley. "The daily texture of Utopian life," a revealing passage reads, "was woven of various and interesting foods and drinks, of free and entertaining exercise and work, of sweet sleep and of the interest and happiness of fearless and spiteless love-making."[6] That last item about the love-making, especially, evokes one of the principal features of Fordian civilization.

Barnstaple himself has no importance for *Brave New World*, except insofar as his solitary condition at the end of the novel suggests that of the Savage. Ironically, Barnstaple, bald, pudgy, middle-aged, and married, suffers from neglect where the Savage ails from surfeit. "The loveliness of the Utopian girls and women," Wells rather sympathetically observes, "who glanced at him curiously or passed him with a serene indifference, crushed down his self-respect and made the Utopian world altogether intolerable to him."[7] No fearless and spiteless love-making for him, alas. But one of the other earthlings does seem to have a more vital counnection to Huxley's satire, a certain Rupert Catskill who is a thinly veiled caricature of Winston Churchill. Catskill is the most energetic and articulate devil's advocate in the novel. He roundly denounces the serenity of the Utopians to their own faces, calls theirs a life unfit for heroes, lacking in drama and opportunity to experience man's full potential. Eventually he even seizes an outlying castle and proposes to fight to the finish against a degenerate future.

Catskill and his companions, including Freddy Mush (Edward Marsh) and Lord Barralonga (Lord Beaverbrook), are clearly meant to be throwbacks to a feudal past (hence the castle). And of course they are meant to be ridiculous. So they are, but in the event only marginally more so than their opponents. And here appears another parallel to Huxley's world: Catskill's objections to utopia resemble closely those of the Savage, and like Catskill the Savage also makes an attempt to overthrow the established authority, and also prefers the past to the future. Perhaps even the lighthouse to which the Savage retires may be intended as an echo of Catskill's castle. And if so, then we are faced with the somewhat mind-boggling prospect of young Winston as the sire of a New Mexican savage.

However, more even than *Men Like Gods*, *Brave New World* resembles *When the Sleeper Wakes*. Like Huxley's novel, this work is also more an attack on, than an idealization of the future. "Here was no Utopia, no Socialistic state," the Sleeper is made to realize early in this novel. Without entering into the details of its rather absurd, Bellamy-like plot, one can say that the whole quality of the civilization it depicts is quite Fordian. The countryside, for instance, has disappeared from consciousness altogether and daily life has become exclusively urban. The "squat" building of thirty-four stories that sets the scene for the opening of *Brave New World* would fit in nicely here. So would the attitude, at any rate among the managing class, to pleasure and sex. There are, for instance, the so-called Pleasure Cities, "strange places, reminiscent of the legendary Sybaris, cities of art and beauty, sterile wonderful cities of motion and music, whither repaired all who profited by the fierce, inglorious, economic struggle that went on in the glaring labyrinth below." Like the Savage, the Sleeper is repelled (and fascinated) by the sexual license of the new world, refusing offers to inspect a pleasure city more intimately. Like the Savage again, he despises women who make advances. He wants a woman to love rather than merely make love to. And like the Savage he resists all attempts to tamper with the essence of his personality. Invited to submit to the local hypnotic personality controllers, the Sleeper refuses, preferring "very keenly to remain absolutely himself." Similarly, the bosses of the new bureaucracy, the "prominent officers of the Food Trust" and "the controller of the European Piggeries" leave him as unimpressed as the Arch-Songster of Canterbury does the Savage.[8] What they both value is depth of experience, rather than breadth, and for them the two are mutually exclusive. In the jargon of contemporary sociology, they are inner-directed.

When the Sleeper Wakes also contains a remarkable series of technological anticipations of the Fordian world, many of which have been catalogued by Mark Hillegas.[9] There is an "International Crèche Syndicate" which falls half-way between a day-care center and a Hatchery and Conditioning Center; there are even infant "incubating cases," a feature that the Sleeper finds particularly disgusting; and there is transatlantic transport vaguely analogous to Huxley's passenger rockets, along with "babble machines" to drum propaganda into the captive minds of the masses. One could go farther, as Hillegas has done, and ransack other Wells novels for more similarities. In A Modern Utopia, criminals and deviants are exiled to islands, much as in Huxley's novel; and in The First Men in the Moon (1901), there is a termitelike society in which "every citizen knows his place. He is born to that place, and the elaborate discipline of training and education and surgery he undergoes fits him at last so completely to it that he has neither ideas nor organs for any purpose beyond it."[10] Even Huxley's free-martins are matched by the large majority of neuter Selenites.

It is clear that Huxley borrowed a number of the technological aspects of his utopia from Wells, but it would be dangerous to

conclude that Wells was Huxley's primary source of scientific information. In the immediate Huxley background, as we have seen,
were his brother Julian and various sometime friends such as
J. B. S. Haldane and Bertrand Russell. And in any case, the technological details, whether Wellsian or no, are not what matter
most. These are only the most superficially memorable aspects of
Huxley's novel, and as he himself soon realized he had blundered
badly by missing out on one of the most obvious ones, atomic
energy. But while this omission is surprising, it certainly does not
vitiate the continuing force of his satire. Is Swift's *Gulliver's
Travels* no longer of interest because a thorough exploration of the
globe has turned up no islands inhabited by Houyhnhnms?

"I would be easy," Huxley wrote in 1931, no doubt a little self-
consciously, "but quite uninteresting to catalogue the errors of past
prophets. The only significant parts of their prognostications, the
only parts of them which we can usefully compare with contemporary prophesyings, are the forecasts of political and social organization. Coaches may give place to airplanes, but man remains very
much what he was—a mainly gregarious animal endowed with a
certain number of anti-social instincts. Whatever tools he uses,
however slowly or quickly he may travel, he must always be governed and regimented" (*Music at Night* 149–50). Despite all the
gadgetry, in other words, the proper study of the novelist remains
man. That is why a remark like Gerald Heard's about *Brave New
World's* being "obsolete because of the growth and findings of
subsequent research" seems quite beside the point.[11]

Huxley, it is true, made no secret of his suspicion of democracy
and of the machine, especially when in combination—as, for instance, in Scogan's remarks on this subject in *Crome Yellow* or the
essay "Revolutions" in *Do What You Will* (1929). After his first
traumatic experience of the U.S.A. in 1926, that suspicion grew
even more intense. But surely not, as Mark Hillegas asserts, for
selfish reasons.[12] After all, a great deal of Huxley's intellectual and
artistic life prior to *Brave New World* (and following it) was taken
up with the effort to find an adequate solution to the wearisome
condition of this chiefly gregarious but intermittently anti-social
creature called man. *Brave New World* is no exception. It is no
mere what-would-it-be-like-if-pigs-could-fly fantasy, but a bitter
attack on a kind of mentality that was seeking to destroy man and

replace him with an anthropoid beast or an anthropoid machine. That after all was the point of the epigraph that Huxley had chosen for his novel from Berdyaev's *The End of Our Time* (1927).

In one of Huxley's earlier novels, *Point Counter Point*, there is a description of a painting by a character named Mark Rampion (based on D. H. Lawrence) that depicts the evolution of man. It begins with a minuscule monkey and passes, via various stages of primitive man, through Greece, Rome, and the Renaissance, with the figures growing ever larger as they approximate the present. "The crescendo continued uninterrupted through Watt and Stevenson, Faraday and Darwin, Bessemer and Edison, Rockefeller and Wanamaker to come to a contemporary consummation in the figures of Mr. H. G. Wells and Sir Alfred Mond. Nor was the future neglected. Through the radiant mist of prophecy the forms of Wells and Mond, growing larger and larger at every repetition, wound in a triumphant spiral clean off the paper, toward Utopian infinity" (290–91). Needless to say, Lawrence never painted such a picture, though as we shall see there was something in Lawrence that makes it appropriate for Huxley to have attributed it to him. The most obvious allusion here is to Wells's *Outline of History* (1920) which, as A. J. P. Taylor has remarked, tries heroically and fails dismally to trace an evolutionary moral "progress" in the history of mankind. Less obviously, there is another allusion—one that explains the otherwise rather puzzling linkage of Wells to Sir Alfred Mond—to *William Clissold* (1926), the massive novel in which Wells first broached his notion of an "Open Conspiracy." This romantic idea of having the modern movers and makers of business and politics combine to seize power and create the World State represented something of a departure from Wells's usual brand of nonconformist socialism. But then there had always been in Wells a kind of permanently adolescent admiration for the sheer daring and imagination of the capitalist entrepreneur—witness the rather mixed feelings with which the Ponderevo business empire is treated in *Tono-Bungay* (1909). Besides, Wells's disillusion in *William Clissold* is not so much with the ideals of socialism as with the sorry lot of ineffective sentimentalists who are identified with it. "Clissold's direction," John Maynard Keynes noted in his review of the book, "is to the Left—far, far to the Left; but he seeks to summon from the Right the creative force and the constructive will which is to carry him there."[13]

Without mentioning him specifically and by name, it was clear that Wells had a man like Alfred Mond in mind for the job of chief open conspirator. Mond came from a distinguished scientific and financial family; his father had founded the highly successful Mond Nickel Company, partially on the basis of scientific discoveries of his own; his brother, Sir Robert Ludwig Mond, was a distinguished chemist and administrator. Alfred Mond himself expanded his father's company into one of the largest and most powerful industrial enterprises in Britain and eventually fused it and other related concerns in 1926 into Imperial Chemical Industries, which, after Ford Motor Company, was probably the largest privately owned corporation in the world. But Mond was not satisfied to remain a mere businessman. He also pursued a successful political career, serving as an MP from 1906 to 1928, first as a Liberal and later as a Tory. He fitted Clissold's bill precisely, all the more so because, despite his conservatism, he was known to favor such progressive ideas as profit sharing and because he attributed his success, above all, to his ability to make his workers believe that his interest was also their own.

That Huxley was not alone in associating Wells's name with Mond's is evident from Philip Gibbs's *The Day After Tomorrow* (1927). According to Gibbs, Wells "seems to have lost faith in the advance of democracy to a flower-strewn Utopia with Men like Gods, and in his recent work [*William Clissold*] suggests that human progress can only be attained by an intellectual aristocracy of very rich men, remarkably like Sir Alfred Mond, who will create enormous trusts, discipline the lower classes, and create a new heaven on earth by scientific organization and divinely inspired committee meetings."[14]

There is no first-hand evidence that Huxley had read *William Clissold*. The only novel of Wells, aside from the scientific fantasies, that Huxley mentions in his correspondence or in his (prophetic) essay "If My Library Burned Tonight," is *Tono-Bungay*, and he found that disappointing. That he had some knowledge of *William Clissold* is, however, strongly suggested by his connection

of Wells with Mond. But if he had not read the novel, what was the
source of his knowledge? The answer, I think, is provided by *Point
Counter Point:* from D. H. Lawrence.

Lawrence had not merely read *William Clissold;* he had reviewed it—though only the first volume—in 1926 for the *Calendar
of Modern Letters*. He condemns the latter half of the book as a
duller résumé of the *Outline of History* in words that seem to
presage Rampion's drawing: "Cave men, nomads, patriarchs, tribal
Old Men, out they all come again, in the long march of human
progress. Mr. Clissold, who holds forth against 'system,' cannot
help systematising us all into a gradual and systematic uplift from
the ape."[15] Lawrence's verdict was that Wells's novel was not a
work of art, which in a way is odd because Lawrence was generaly
sympathetic to Wells, in part because he felt that he and Wells had
had similar social obstacles to face and overcome. Perhaps what
Lawrence resented here even more than Wells's lack of art was his
glorification of the modern businessman.

It is tempting to think of Lawrence and Huxley discussing and
condemning Wells together, especially the Wells of *William Clissold;* but agains there is no real evidence that they did. There is
only the hint of *Point Counter Point* and, even more tantalizing,
the poem "Wellsian Futures" in *Pansies* (1929):

> When men are made in bottles
> and emerge as squeaky globules with no bodies to speak of,
> and therefore nothing to have feelings with,
>
> they will still squeak intensely about their feelings
> and be prepared to kill you if you say you've got none.[16]

What makes this poem especially interesting with regard to Huxley
(aside from the fact that *Brave New World* contradicts it outright) is
that there is nothing about babies made in bottles anywhere in
Wells. Huxley, on the other hand, had already raised the possibility twice, once in *Crome Yellow* and again in *Proper Studies* (1927),
and Lawrence had certainly read the latter book. There is more
than a slight possibility, therefore, that Lawrence got the scientific
information for his poem from Huxley. As it happens, there is
circumstantial evidence to support this hypothesis in Julian Huxley's *Memories* (1970), where Huxley's brother mentions lively dis-

cussions of "evolutionary and physiological ideas, including the idea of mankind's genetic improvement."[17] These discussions took place at Diablerets in the winter of 1927–28, when Lawrence was also present. In fact it was almost certainly at one of these sessions that Lawrence delivered his famous outburst against evolution.

If what I have argued here is true, then Lawrence bears a considerable, if indirect responsibility for the figure of Mond/Wells in *Brave New World*. Nor is that his only responsibility. In an essay, rather oddly entitled "Man Must Work and Woman as Well" (November 1929), Lawrence examines what he sees as the modern anti-work ethic. Progress, for modern men and women, has come to mean less work and more pay. No longer is there pride or joy in creation through work. The new ethic is the ethic of enjoyment, with more films, dances, golf, tennis and "more getting completely away from yourself." This, according to Lawrence, is the "plan of the universe laid down by the great magnates of industry like Mr. Ford."

Science and technology, however, have not been able to keep pace with the new ethic. The abstract desire for increased enjoyment is frustrated by the practical reality of inadequate labor-saving machinery. There is not even a satisfactory mechanical dishwasher, much less "babies bred in bottles and food in tabloid form." As a consequence, there is an enormous resentment at having to remain physical and laborious when one so ardently wishes to be mechanical and "joyous."

The new ethic also has an inevitable impact on the old moral and social order. Traditional institutions like marriage and the family are withering away along with the old work ethic. There is a fundamental change in instinct. Sexuality turns into promiscuity. People turn away from actual reality in favor of a pseudo-reality mediated by machines: "We don't *want* to look at flesh and blood people— we want to watch their shadows on a screen. We don't *want* to hear their actual voices: only transmitted through a machine. We must get away from the physical."[18]

The connection of these ideas with *Brave New World* is obvious. They are not, of course, ideas that are original with Lawrence. With a few changes of emphasis and chronological context, they could easily have been stated by Carlyle or Ruskin. But originality is not the point here. The point is that Lawrence was intensely

preoccupied with the deterioration of the social and moral nature
of modern man in ways that closely resemble Huxley's own preoccupations. This similarity of viewpoint—with an identical focus in
several striking instances: ectogenesis, the compulsion for enjoyment, the mechanization of man, the substitution of sensation for
feeling—suggests a close interchange on these subjects between
Lawrence and Huxley, an interchange that surely did not move
only in one direction.

Lawrence also exercised another and quite different influence on
Brave New World. For just as behind Mond and behind the whole
technological world that he controls stands H. G. Wells, so behind
the Savage and the New Mexican Pueblo stands D. H. Lawrence.

When Huxley began work on *Brave New World*, he had never
been to New Mexico. That he had not seems in fact to have
troubled him, since nearly thirty years later he recalled having
"had to do an enormous amount of reading up on New Mexico,
because I'd never been there. I read all sorts of Smithsonian reports on the place and then did the best I could to imagine it."[19] His
path passed near New Mexico a couple of years later during the
travels described in *Beyond the Mexique Bay* (1934), but he did not
actually set foot there until 1937.

If, however, Huxley had not been to New Mexico and if, for that
reason, he had to do a good deal of boning up on it, one wonders
why he bothered. If it was underdeveloped or non-Western
societies he was after, he had already seen several such during his
travels in the Far East in 1926. Why then? Perhaps in order to
have a peculiarly American locale to match the American flavor of
the Fordian world? Yes, possibly, though this suggestion still does
not account specifically for New Mexico. Why not Arizona instead,
or even Texas or Florida, or any other American state with a sizable
Indian population?

The real answer is Lawrence. By the time Huxley came to know
him intimately, Lawrence had already, to be sure, closed the New
Mexican chapter of his life, but he had by no means forgotten it.
"In later years," Huxley wrote in his preface to Knud Merrild's *A
Poet and Two Painters* (1938), a memoir about Lawrence in New
Mexico by a Dane who had lived there with him, "he [Lawrence]
often talked of the place—talked with a mixture of love and dislike;
nostalgically longing to be back in that ferociously virgin world of

drought and storm, and at the same time resenting its alienness and lunar vacancy."[20] New Mexico, it seems safe to assume, existed for Huxley (that is, before he delved into the Smithsonian reports) only insofar as he had heard from it from Lawrence.

Lawrence, however, did not merely talk about New Mexico; he had also written of it. Though he saved his best energies for the old Mexico—much to the dismay of Mabel Dodge-Luhan who had lured him to Taos to be a sort of combined poet-in-residence and genius loci—he did compose several impressionistic sketches about the Indians and landscape of New Mexico.

The sketch that seems most immediately relevant to the Pueblo section of *Brave New World* is entitled "The Hopi Snake Dance," and it gives Lawrence's reaction to the most dramatic of all the Pueblo Indian dances. The outward trappings of the dance seemed to Lawrence merely spectacular circus tricks with snakes dangling from the performers' mouths but he was profoundly impressed by the gripping rhythmic nature of the ritual, symbolized by the continuous beating of the drum and the pad of human feet. Here was the real heart of the Indian, Lawrence thought; here was his eternal assertion that god and life are one.

The other sketches play variations on much the same theme, usually with a heavy accompaniment of the percussion instruments. Not that Lawrence naively idealizes the life of the Indian. He aggressively demands the "debunking" of the Indian and maintains that "it is almost impossible for the white people to approach the Indian without either sentimentality or dislike."[21] Even so, one suspects that Lawrence felt that he himself had managed to achieve the nearly impossible. Certainly he felt that he had made contact with something that was older and stranger and more godlike than anything he had known before. "I had no permanent feeling of religion," he writes in "New Mexico," "till I came to New Mexico and penetrated into the old human race-experience there." And elsewhere in the same essay he even goes as far as to say that "New Mexico was the greatest experience from the outside world that I ever had. It certainly changed me forever. Curious as it may sound, it was New Mexico that liberated me from the present era of civilization, the great era of material and mechanical development."[22]

Understatement was, of course, not Lawrence's strong point,

but undoubtedly New Mexico left its mark on him. For a brief period Lawrence even convinced himself that he was an integral part of New Mexico, living high up on his ranch, surrounded by his women and his cow, with the Indians just a few steps away. This is probably the New Mexico about which Lawrence "often" spoke to Huxley, for no matter how strenuously Lawrence might have wished to debunk the Indian, he was an iconophile, not an iconoclast. It was Huxley who was the debunker.

There are signs that Huxley was debunking Lawrence even when their friendship was at its height. Lawrence must have been at least partly on his mind when Huxley wrote in "The Cold-Blooded Romantics" (1928) that "the modern artist seems to have grown down; he has reverted to the preoccupation of his childhood. He is trying to be a primitive. So, it may be remembered, was the romantic Rousseau. But whereas Rousseau's savage was noble, refined, and intelligent, the primitive our modern artists would like to resemble is a mixture between the apache and the fifteen-year old schoolboy."[23] Reading this, one is reminded of the scene in "Indians and the Englishman" where Lawrence is confronted in the dusk by an Apache who, he is convinced, wishes to murder him. Here they are, the twin spirits of Lawrence: Natty Bumppo and the primitive blood-consciousness.

Certainly by the time Huxley was writing *Brave New World*, he was sure that Lawrence's primitive utopia no longer cut any ice, or at any rate no more than Wells's technological one. "In beating the West with an extreme-oriental stick, contemporary writers like Lowes Dickinson and Bertrand Russell have only revived a most respectable literary tradition," Huxley observed in 1931. "The primitive and prehistoric Utopias of D. H. Lawrence and [Grafton] Elliot Smith have as good a pedigree. Our ancestors knew all about the State of Nature and the Noble Savage." It had all been tried before and had failed, so runs the implication, so why try and fail again? Here Lawrence's utopian vision is degraded (or should one say debunked?) to the point of being just another literary stone piled on an already ruinous edifice. Later on in the essay, Lawrence is degraded even further, to the level of a fad (as he is in *Eyeless in Gaza*). "With every advance of industrial civilization," Huxley predicts, "the savage past will be more and more appreciated, and the cult of D. H. Lawrence's *Dark God* may be expected to spread through an ever-widening circle of worship-pers" (*Music at Night*, 141–42, 147). Now Lawrence is the fashion-able cultist, no longer the prophet of a new religion. And now the connection is made explicit: Lawrence *is* the savage past.

The savage past or the Fordian future? That is the question which *Brave New World* poses. The Malpais (literally "bad coun-try" in Spanish) of prehistory or the ironically "Buenpais" of post-history? The choice is between two evils. Not that Lawrence is to be exclusively identified with the one or Wells with the other; that would be to simplify excessively the complexity of Huxley's vision, and to err by trying to make a partial truth do the work of a whole one. Huxley's Pueblo Indians, closely related as they are to Law-rence's, also have other ancestors. The fragmentary tales they tell derive, for instance, not from Lawrence but from Frank Cushing's *Zuñi Folk Tales* (1901), which seems also to be the source of many of Huxley's Indian names, including Mitsima and Waihusiva, not to mention the Smithsonian reports.[24]

No, though Lawrence's experience of New Mexico and Law-rence's antipathy to science, to social regimentation, and to pro-miscuous sexuality surely helped shape the spirit of the Savage, it would be wrong to identify him with Lawrence too completely. For one thing, it is important to note that Huxley transformed the Pueblo Indians, in one respect at least, almost as much as he did our own world. The Pueblo Indians—as the Smithsonian reports, among others, make clear—are anthropologically a separate entity from the Penitentes. According to Elsie Clewes Parsons's massive study of Pueblo Indian religion—not published in book form until 1939 but a considerable proportion of which had already appeared as articles by the end of the twenties—the Penitentes are "an organization [that] the Indians observe with interest as comparable to their own esoteric groups."[25] But there is no mingling of the two, certainly nothing like the fusion that exists in *Brave New World*. Huxley was, of course, aware of this fact and in his foreword de-scribed the religion of his Indians as "half fertility cult and half *Penitente* ferocity" (p. viii).

The fertility cult is Indian and, as one might expect, the snake dance is part of that cult. How closely this feature of Pueblo Indian life was linked with Lawrence in Huxley's mind may be appreciated from H. K. Haeberlin's observation that "the Great Serpent of the Pueblo is commonly known as the 'plumed serpent.'" So too with the *sipapus*, the openings in the floor of the *kiva*, which play an important part in Huxley's description of the snake dance. It is there that the deities of germination and fertility reside. And associated with these deities are also the wargods, "Püükon and his less important [twin] brother."[26]

"Püükon" is obviously Huxley's Pookong, but in *Brave New World* his twin brother has been replaced by Christ, and along with Christ have also come the Penitentes. To be sure, there are certain points of historical contact between the native Indian rites and those of the Penitentes, some of which may possibly derive from Spanish influence at the time of the Conquest. Both groups practice fasting, continence, and flagellation. The use of emetics is, however, a peculiarly Indian custom, and, though the Indians do practice whipping, it is very mild indeed compared to the Penitentes. The Pueblo Indians would certainly never tolerate sadism of the kind that climaxes the snake dance in *Brave New World*. Their whippings take place at initiation ceremonies only and then always in groups, with each youth accompanied by an adult sponsor who is sometimes also whipped. The maximum number of strokes is usually four and there is no attempt on the part of the person being struck to conceal pain. Furthermore, no Pueblo Indian would go out alone into the desert and commit an act such as the Savage describes. "Once," he tells Bernard Marx, "I did something that none of the others did: I stood against a rock in the middle of the day, in summer, with my arms out, like Jesus on the Cross" (93).

What is Huxley's point here? Why does he insist on combining an Indian fertility cult with a Christian penitential ritual? If it is merely to suggest that the forces of life are balanced by those of death—Huxley, one remembers, is often accused of Manichaeanism—then he could have portrayed that balance with much less effort by means of the Aztecs of the Old Mexico. Sir James Frazer's *Sacrificial God* is full of horrific examples.

Then why? Because, I suspect, he wishes to make a point about the relation of life to death that he could not have done using the Aztecs. The Aztecs practiced human sacrifice in order to preserve the life of their gods; for them death was merely another aspect of fertility. This is one of the chief reasons why Lawrence rooted his dark god in the *old* Mexican soil. But here again Huxley is debunking Lawrence. Life, Huxley implies, is life, never to be confused with death—unless it is the everlasting life, the life beyond death. Lawrence, as Huxley knew, disliked Christianity and may have feared it. Characteristically, he tried to shut himself off from all contact with the Penitentes during his stay in Taos. As Eliot Fay, who was in Taos at the same time as Lawrence, recalled years later, he would close the windows of his room whenever the Penitentes began their evening chants and cries.[27]

There is another and perhaps more important reason why Huxley may have chosen to put the Penitentes into his novel. *Brave New World* portrays a future and a past that differ from the present in that they have no history. Our Ford's remark that "History is bunk" applies with equal force to the Pueblo and to the London of A.F. 632. Both are stable societies that can tolerate no change and therefore possess no history. Now, the one relatively stable institution known to the West in modern historical times is the Church. Significantly, Christianity is the most important shared element of both the Fordian and the Pueblo societies.

This may be less apparent in the new world, but it is no less true. The Solidarity Service that forms a counterpart of the Pueblo Snake Dance is an obvious parody of the mass. The loving-cup of strawberry ice-cream soma is based on the bread and wine of the holy communion. ("All the advantages of Christianity and alcohol; none of their defects" (36), is how Mustapha Mond defines soma). The Solidarity hymns appear to echo Wesley's, and there is even an oblique reference to the Holy Spirit in the "enormous negro dove" at the close of the service. Like the Snake Dance, the Solidarity Service also has an underlying sexual meaning, though here it would be more appropriate to call it a sterility rite. When the drums begin to beat at the Reservation, Lenina's first thought is of the Solidarity Services. " 'Orgy-porgy,' she whispered to herself. These drums beat out just the same rhythm" (75).

Christianity is an essential element in both of the worlds Huxley depicts. But—and this is a crucial distinction—it is not the same Christianity. In the one instance, it is the Christianity that maintains that we inhabit a vale of tears and that we should mortify the flesh in this life in order to store up credit in the next; on the other,

it is the Christianity that promises a paradise on earth. The one is
Christianity in rags, with flagellation and retreats into the desert;
the other Christianity in riches, with everybody "happy" and the
peace of the world insured by ten semi-apostolic World Controllers. "Suffer little children" (38), Mustapha Mond admonishes the
DHC who has disturbed the little girls and boys at their erotic
play.[28]

At the end of *Brave New World*, secular and fanatic Christianity
meet and join. The Savage's flagellation of himself and Lenina,
echoing the dance at the Pueblo, merges with the orgy-porgy
dance of the visiting Fordians and culminates in a fertility-sterility
rite in which the Savage finally yields his principles and himself.
The only purification for that sin, he realizes on the following day,
is death. Such is the result of the Controller's "experiment." Pueblo is Pueblo, and Ford is Ford, and ne'er the twain shall meet, for
if they do disaster ensues. Stability lies at the extremes, not at the
middle; in machine and in monster, not in man. The choice is
between the chiliastic horrors of the Wellsian future or those of the
Lawrentian past, both of which exclude the (by comparison lesser)
day-to-day trauma of Huxleyan—or human—present.

And what does Huxley mean to suggest by all this? Perhaps, as
he once wrote to his brother Julian, "all's well that ends Wells" (L.
103). To which he might later have added that finishing off Lawrence, as a social philosopher at least, was not a bad idea either.

4

The Politics of Anti-Utopia

Faustian man has become a *slave of his creation*. His number, and the arrangement of life as he sees it, have been driven by the machine into a path where there is no standing still and no turning back. The peasant, the hand-worker, even the merchant, appear suddenly as inessential in comparison with the *three great figures that the Machine has bred and trained up in the cause of its development: the entrepreneur, the engineer, and the factory-worker*.

Oswald Spengler, *The Decline of the West*

Indeed scientific knowledge has not merely heightened the possibilities of life in the modern world, it has lowered the depths. When science is not touched by a sense of values it works—as it fairly consistently has worked during the past century—towards a complete dehumanization of the social order.

Lewis Mumford, *The Story of Utopias*

In the summer of 1931, while Huxley was writing *Brave New World*, Britain verged on economic and political disaster. The Labour Government fell, the pound fell, productivity fell, unemployment rose, riots broke out in London and Glasgow, the Navy mutinied at Invergordon, long lines formed everywhere, and the depression settled down over Britain like an ominous cloud. The crisis that had been sweeping through Europe since the Great War and through the United States since the Great Crash of 1929 was about to engulf Britain as well.

Into this very unbrave world, less than a year later, Aldous

Huxley launched his anti-utopian novel. It was to prove an immediate success, but it left at least one of its first readers puzzled. What, Granville Hicks wondered out loud, was the point of publishing an anti-utopian novel at a time like this? A novel set in a future so remote that it had virtually nothing to do with the present crisis and whose only political concern was something so irrelevant as stability? Surely there were other and more important things to write about than this?[1]

In the bleak decade that followed, others took up Hicks' reproach: *Brave New World*, for all its brilliance, had precious little to offer anyone seeking political instruction. For H. G. Wells, the author of *Brave New World* was "a brilliant reactionary." So too for J. D. Bernal, but without the qualifying epithet. Harold Laski announced that Huxley was, politically speaking, a flop, for he had "never seriously confronted, in novel or in essay, the burning issues which are destroying the very foundations of our social system." And shortly after the Second World War, George Orwell concluded that, compared with Evgenii Zamiatin's *We*, *Brave New World* "shows less political awareness."[2]

With these verdicts some scholars have tended subsequently to agree. According to Judith Shklar, *Brave New World* "is not a political novel and offers no insights into totalitarian systems." Less categorical, more personal, but equally stringent is Mark Hillegas, who argues that *Brave New World* is the product of "a cynical, bored young man who . . . was against utopia not only because it would mechanize human life but because it would give abundance and leisure to everyone, making these no longer the special privilege of people like himself."[3]

Is this true? Is it true that *Brave New World* is either apolitical or, even worse, cynically reactionary? Does it shed no light whatever on the totalitarian revolutions—from the right and from the left—that have been the bane of twentieth-century political life? Is the novel simply the result of upper-class reluctance to share one's pleasures with the poor?

If to be political a novel must be based on some specific political incident, like Arthur Koestler's *Darkness at Noon*, or on a specific political system, like George Orwell's *Animal Farm*, then *Brave New World* is not political. There is in the novel no immediately

visible connection either between the events or the society it describes and any actually existing political state. Ergo, *Brave New
World* cannot be political. But by the same token, Plato's *Republic*
is not a political book, for it too has no direct link with any state that
has ever existed. To any sensible critic, I think, the absurdity of
defining politics in this Procrustean way must be apparent. Politics
is not simply the politics of a particular moment or place; nor is
politics simply the sum of the activity of politicians. Politics rather
is everything that has to do with the behavior and organization of
men into groups, especially in large groups, such as cities or states.
Understood this way, politics certainly plays a very important role
in *Brave New World*.

There are plenty of political signals in Huxley's novel. Take, for
example, the opening paragraph. The short first sentence—"A
squat grey building of only thirty-four storeys"—at once conveys
the point of view of a "sophisticated" urbanite, the inhabitant of a
polis for whom it is possible for a thirty-four-story building to be
squat. Implicit in the sentence is a world of megalopolises and
population concentration that make the London of 1932 seem almost like a village. The second sentence—the opening paragraph
contains only two (fragmentary) sentences—is even richer in political overtones: "Over the main entrance the worlds, CENTRAL
LONDON HATCHERY AND CONDITIONING CENTRE, and,
in a shield, the World State's motto, COMMUNITY, IDENTITY,
STABILITY." These two inscriptions cannot be deciphered by the
reader entirely at this point and properly so, for Huxley's wants to
arouse the reader's curiosity. But even to the uninitiated the existence of a combined hatchery and conditioning center in the middle of London must carry some meaning. Regardless of whether
chickens or humans or something else is being hatched and conditioned here, the very existence of this kind of institution in this
kind of place must presuppose a politically very different society
from the one we live in now. This suspicion is confirmed by the fact
that there is a "World State" and that this state has a motto that is
very different from, but at the same time invokes, the motto of the
French Revolutionary state: Liberty, Equality, Fraternity. The
ideals of the world state are clearly not the ideals of traditional
European political democracy, though they appear to be related in

some, possibly ironic way to those ideals. We sense, by the time we have finished reading the first paragraph, that we have entered a strangely altered political world.

As we delve farther into the novel, we are quickly enlightened about some of the salient features of the new world state: genetic control and predestination; rigid caste system; total social and political conditioning; rampant economic consumerism; pacification through drugs; political power concentrated in the hands of a few controllers. This, in rough outline, is the sociopolitical structure of the new world state. We are made aware of this framework indirectly and in bits and pieces; the reader must assemble those pieces himself if he wishes to have an overview of the political world. Huxley does not do it for him, nor should he, for *Brave New World* is after all a novel and not a systematic political treatise. Precisely because Huxley never forgets that he is writing a novel, because he refuses to hector his reader with statistics and blueprints, he succeeds in implanting in his reader's mind the basic political facts of the new world in an entirely natural way. We are actually made to enter the new world; we do not simply learn about it.

How "natural" this world is can be gauged by its closeness, for all the manifold differences, to our own world. Unlike most utopias or even anti-utopias—Wells' *Men Like Gods* or Butler's *Erewhon*, for example—*Brave New World* does not begin with the intrusion of a stranger into the new world, who is then introduced to its wonders, amid much lecturing and condescension. Why does Huxley fail to use this ancient device? Because it is so ancient? Or because by virtue of this omission we are made to sense that we need no introduction to this new world, since it is only another version of our own world. When the intruder finally does appear it is in the guise of the Savage, and the reader is already thoroughly familiar with the new world. The intruder's function, therefore, is very different: to shock us into an awareness of the monstrosity of a world that is in many ways the mirror image of our own, and that, because of this similarity, we may be in danger of accepting.

Despite its grotesque name and despite the more than grotesque nature of its business, the routine of the Central London Hatchery and Conditioning Centre is very much like the routine of any large twentieth-century corporation, such as, for example, the Ford

Motor Company. There is the product; there are the workers who need to be supervised; there is management; there is the new personnel that needs to be trained. Nor is there anything, on the surface at least, static about this vast corporation. It is not as if everything were always the same. Mistakes are made: fetuses are given alcohol when they should not, or necessary injections are unwittingly omitted. Greater perfection is aimed at: more buds out of ovaries, more complete cloning procedures. All this seems very "human" and familiar.

Familiar too are the "individuals" and the "personal" life within the corporation: the eager-beaver management type represented by Henry Foster or, in maturer form, by the Director of Hatcheries and Conditioning; the popular girl, Lenina, fashionable and desirable, but not quite conforming to the official sexual code; another girl, Fanny, less popular and attractive, more conventional, given to pious platitudes and "moral" exhortations; finally the misfit, Bernard Marx, who has difficulty adjusting satisfactorily to both his public and personal roles. All of these people are part of the same corporation and belong to the same caste groups—Alpha in the case of the men; Beta in that of the two women—but their appearance is quite different, and their personalities and abilities vary markedly. These differences do not necessarily make them individuals. To be an individual there has to be a sense of separate identity, a sense lacking in almost all of the inhabitants of the new world. But the differences do make them distinctive and distinguishable, at least to the same degree as most twentieth-century people in equivalent positions would be distinguishable.

What is important to note here is that these new world people are, *mutatis mutandis*, perfectly ordinary old world people: ambitious, petty, hard-minded, dreamy, lazy, afraid, snobbish, sometimes unconventional, occasionally defiant, full of gossip, bored. These are people, not machines, even though they are people who have been bred by machines. They are perfectly ordinary people: that, indeed, is the problem, for in the old world it was possible for perfectly extraordinary people to exist. This is not the case in the new.

Still, the inhabitants of the new world are people, not supermen or walking radios. This is an important political point: whatever man makes, even if it is man himself, will remain imperfect. It is

the reassuring gap between the "ideal" and the practical achievement of that ideal in the new world state that allows for the appearance of potentially extraordinary people like Bernard Marx and
Helmholtz Watson. No political system, not even that of the new
world state, is airtight.

This is true, but it is also true that the new world comes as close
as possible to excluding all political freedom. In the new world
state only the Controllers are able to affect directly the political
conditions of their existence, and, what is more to the point, only
to those ten—and to isolated misfits like Marx and Watson—could
it ever occur to try to alter those conditions. The ideal way of
wielding political power is to make that power invisible; that is, to
obliterate, not the power itself, but the ability to perceive or even
to conceive of that power. This is what the withering-away of the
state means in Huxley's new world; and it is precisely this that
permits Mustapha Mond to wander out among his charges like a
shepherd among his flock. Sheep have never been known to rise
up against their masters.

The relationship of the shepherd to his sheep is an ancient and
much honored one. Inevitably it evokes biblical analogies of the
Good Shepherd and of his concern for the lost lamb. These images
are not wholly inappropriate to Mustapha Mond, whom we first
encounter caring for the education of his new "lambs." Mond is the
closest the new world comes to the triumphant Christ—to that
traditional version of a "man-like-god"—just as the Savage is this
world's only possible approximation to the suffering Christ, or god-
like-man. It is Mond, the good shepherd, who allows the Savage,
the lost lamb of this particular parable, to rejoin his kind in the new
world. Mond is a good shepherd; and all the better, in fact, for
differing from other good shepherds in not periodically slaughter-
ing a portion of his flock. Sheep, one recalls, have been
scientifically bred for longer than any other species of animal, except perhaps dogs.

For Huxley, the shepherd and his sheep, however, also carry
other connotations. As he notes in his long essay on Maine de
Biran, the shepherd is the image of the perfect totalitarian, for he
keeps his herd in utter subservience and watches over them, not
for their own ultimate benefit, but for his own (*Themes and Variations*, 54–55).

This totalitarian aspect of the new world state may explain why the characters bear such an apparently odd assortment of names—names that, more often than not, have very specific and often contradictory political overtones. Among the obviously political names are: [Kemal Ataturk] Mustapha, Turkish nationalist dictator; Primo [de Rivera], Spanish dictator; [Charles] Bradlaugh, Socialist freethinker; Trotsky; Lenin[a]; Marx; Engels; Bakunin; Hoover; Benito [Mussolini]; [Ivan Vasilevich] Bokanovsky, Russian revolutionary; Ford; [Sir Alfred] Mond of Imperial Chemical Industries; and [Andrew] Mellon. These names are drawn from almost the entire range of nineteenth- and twentieth-century politics: from revolutionaries and anarchists (Bokanovsky and Bakunin) to Soviet strongmen (Trotsky and Lenin), to nonviolent socialists (Bradlaugh, Wells, and Shaw), to American presidents and democratic entrepreneurs (Hoover, Ford, Mond, et al.), to fascist and quasi-fascist dictators (Mussolini, Mustapha, Habibullah Khan, and Primo de Rivera). Politically speaking, the only important category not represented here is that of old-fashioned conservatives and aristocrats.

What is the point of this rather confusing array of names? What might Huxley's purpose be in throwing together into one pot political points of view so diametrically opposed as communism, fascism, and democratic capitalism? What do these, separately or collectively, have to do with the new world?

The point that Huxley is making here, I think, is not merely that from the perspective of distant time the concerns of the present fuse together into a single whole. Rather, what Huxley seems to be implying is that all of the dynamic political forces of the twentieth century, no matter how divergent they appear on the surface, are really tending in the same direction, that of the new world state. All of these forces share the claims of "totality," to a final knowledge of the nature of man and of his proper political condition. All are fundamentally materialist, in that they envision man's salvation here on earth: in a reborn Roman Empire or a proletarian paradise or a Ford factory run wild over the whole globe. In this sense they are all utopian. They all glorify machines and modern technology.[4] They all, to a greater or lesser degree, subordinate the individual to the claims of a collective whole: the class, nation, or the business economy. Moreover, aside from these general resemblances, there

seem to be quite specific links between each one of these political
systems of the twentieth century and the new world state: from
fascism comes the caste system; from communism, the emphasis
on conditioning and propaganda; and from democratic capitalism
the economy oriented toward lavish and purposeless production
and consumption.

The new world state, however, possesses a precious quality
which, in Mustapha Mond's view at least, all of its twentieth-
century predecessors lacked, namely, stability. The implication
here may be that the totalitarian states of our time were simply not
totalitarian enough; that they were too ignorant and inefficient to
approximate the smooth, "invisible" functioning of the new world
state. Perhaps, Huxley may be suggesting, only a state—and then
only a "world state"—that combines the various "truths" embodied
in communism, fascism, and capitalist democracy can achieve stability, whereas a state founded on only one of these "truths" is
doomed to instability. Perhaps. What is certain is that the new
world values stability above all else. "Stability," in the words of
Mustapha Mond, "stability. The primal and the ultimate need."
(34). Stability is the foundation on which all else is built, and, not
surprisingly, stability makes a most stable foundation. In a way, of
course, this is true of all utopias and even anti-utopias. Utopias are
not merely "good places" and "no places," but they are also by
definition places where nothing important ever changes, where it
is always business as usual. Utopias, in other words, are set in "no
time" as well as "no place." This is why characters like Marx and
Watson who have reentered time have already departed Utopia,
even before they are officially excluded.

It is this unchanging, eternally stable condition of utopias that
makes them at once so attractive and so terrible. Utopia satisfies
simultaneously our longing for a perfect place and for stasis, and
horrifies us because we realize that the ideal approximation of rest
and stability is death. Hence all utopias are also and always dystopias, and vice-versa. For no matter how disgusted we may be by
the prospect of an eternity of good times in the manner of Huxley's
new world state, there remains a part of us that is drawn to it
nevertheless: because it is permanent, because it has stability,
because it is out of time. Utopias, or more often dystopias, which
exploit this ambiguity of response—as *Brave New World* does and

as *The Republic* does—succeed in touching the imagination more deeply and in a way that more straightforward versions do not.

Historically, of course, no actual political state has ever achieved stability and only a very few have approximated it: prerevolutionary China, for instance, or the institution of the Catholic Church. Even so, it is true to say that this is the aim for which all political states, even the most short-lived, strive, and for which all politicians, even the most pragmatic, plan. In this sense, all existing political units are, teleologically speaking, utopian.

There are, basically, only two ways in which political stability can be achieved, ways that may be conveniently characterized by the carrot and the stick. There is the stability based on anticipating demands and satisfying them, the way of pleasure and the carrot. Then there is the stability based on suppressing demands and eliminating those who make them, the way of terror and the stick. Both ways are represented in *Brave New World*, the former, of course, in the new world state, and the latter—much more fragmentarily—in the New Mexican pueblo. Both are clearly effective, and their coexistence in Huxley's novel seems to suggest that seekers after stability may pay their money and take their choice. To some extent this is true, for clearly the pueblo is brought into the novel as a kind of alternative/mirror-image of the new world state. But it is true only to some extent, for it is also clear that the pueblo exists only at the discretion of the new world state, that it is a kind of zoo for primitives. In terms of numbers and power—political and military—there is no comparison between the two stabilities. Moreover, there is also an implication that the stability of terror can succeed only with a population that is primitive, that it would fail or function only inefficiently (and therefore unstably) if applied to a technologically sophisticated society like the new world state. A modern state has really no choice but to employ the carrot if it wishes to attain stability.

Stability, however, is not merely collective; it is also individual. "Stability," to quote Mustapha Mond again, "stability. No civilization without social stability. No social stability without individual stability" (33). The stability of the whole, in other words, is only as secure as the stability of each of the parts. This is a crucial problem, the answer to which leads Huxley inevitably to the techniques of genetic engineering and psychological conditioning. To achieve collective or social stability one requires individuals whose needs and behavior are completely predictable and therefore controllable. The great difficulty here is that human nature is so complex and variegated that it is almost possible to say that there is no human nature but only human natures. One of Huxley's chief concerns, in the poetry, stories, novels, and essays that he had written prior to *Brave New World,* had been to explore and to some extent catalogue this vast variety of humanity. To assist him in this task he had often turned to psychological theory and had shown a special fondness for psychologists like Kretschmer and Jung—and later W. H. Sheldon—who attempted to correlate psychological and somatic types: to establish, in other words, a science of human natures. *Point Counter Point,* for example, tries to deal systematically—using Kretschmer, Jung, and others—with the strange variety of humanity; it is a kind of novelistic compendium of basic human possibilities.

The problem is even more complicated. Not only are there various differing and sometimes conflicting types of human beings, but each individual human being is either actually or potentially in conflict with himself. The individual is *per se* an unstable entity, torn between altruism and self-interest, between passion and reason: a turmoil of conflicting hopes, appetites, thoughts, instincts. In the words of another "Mustapha"—that of Fulke Greville's play[5]—words that settled deep into Huxley's mind and that he had earlier used as the epigraph to *Point Counter Point:*

> O wearisome condition of humanity!
> Born under one law, to another bound;
> Vainly begot and yet forbidden vanity;
> Created sick, commanded to be sound.
> What meaneth Nature by these diverse laws?
> Passion and reason, self-division's cause.

Self-division and instability, it was evident to Huxley, make up the innately wearisome condition of individual humanity. This being so, it was equally clear that a stable political state could not be founded on a humanity so constituted. The alternative, therefore, was either no political stability, or else the creation of a new and unself-divided type of human being. The latter course is precisely that taken by the founders of the new world state. With political stability as their ultimate aim and value, they could scarcely have acted otherwise.

It is this alteration in human nature and this limitation and standardization of human natures that Huxley means when he writes of the "really revolutionary revolution" in his 1946 foreword to *Brave New World:* "The people who govern the Brave New World may not be sane (in what may be called the absolute sense of the word); but they are not madmen and their aim is not anarchy but social stability. It is in order to achieve stability that they carry out, by scientific means, the ultimate, personal, really revolutionary revolution" (xi). Revolutions hitherto have been superficial, affecting only the outward circumstances of human existence. They have tried to change political constitutions or economic relationships, rather than change the origin of the problem itself: mankind. Only a revolution that takes mankind as its object will really make a difference in social stability; only such a revolution will really deserve the name.

When it comes, so Huxley foresees, the real revolution will be internal and therefore eternal; it will alter the nature of man in order to be able to alter the external conditions of his existence. Only in this way is the creation of a truly stable state possible. That is why Freud must always precede Ford; and that is why Freud—more than anyone else—is the theoretician of the really revolutionary revolution.

In the 1946 foreword, Huxley stipulated that four indispensable conditions had to be met before the really revolutionary revolution could be brought about. These are: (1) "a greatly improved technique of suggestion"; (2) "a fully developed science of human differences"; (3) "a substitute for alcohol and the other narcotics"; and (4) "a foolproof system of eugenics" (xiv). In the new world state all of these conditions are fully satisfied through hypnopaedia and conditioning; social predestination; soma; and genetic engineering. Interestingly enough, the same conditions are also met in Huxley's other novel of the future, *Island*. The really revolutionary revolution, it would appear, can have its winners as well as its losers.

As Huxley's name for it implies, the really revolutionary revolution is conceived in contrast with, but also as a continuation of, earlier and incompletely revolutionary revolutions. One of these revolutionary contrasts/models is obviously the French Revolution of 1789. Both Robespierre and Babeuf are referred to in the foreword, and, as we have seen, the novel itself opens with an evocation of the revolutionary motto, "Liberty, Fraternity, Equality." More important, however, than any of these is the apparently casual reference, late in the novel and in the first name of a very minor character, to Jean Jacques Rousseau. Rousseau, more than any other thinker, was the philosophical force behind the French Revolution; he bears the same relation to it that Freud bears to the really revolutionary revolution. Significantly, Rousseau is also one of the precursors of the more real revolution. According to L. G. Crocker's *Rousseau's Social Contract: An Interpretive Essay*(1968), Rousseau anticipates in his *Social Contract* the idea of total mind control used in the new world state: "Rousseau alone developed the theory that the wielders of political power must capture men's minds, wills, and emotions, and also the essential techniques for doing so." Elsewhere in his study Crocker maintains that Huxley's World Controllers may originate in Rousseau's "Legislator," who is the real totalitarian power behind Rousseau's apparently democratic state.[6] According to another critic, the Legislator is needed because "the people, as Rousseau never forgot, are not very intelligent. It may know its own interests, but it needs help if it is to defend them effectively. Without a legislator to guide them, they will never acquire a character or become aware of themselves as a people."[7]

Rousseau also had a strong anti-intellectual, anti-elitist bias, which was to have evil consequences for the future. He first became famous for his prize-winning attack on the arts and sciences as useless and corrupting *(Discourse on the Arts and Sciences)*, and this view continued to be a leading theme throughout much of his best work. In the novel *Émile*, for example, we are told that "if all the kings and all the philosophers were removed they would scarcely be missed and things would be none the worse";[8] and in another novel, *La Nouvelle Héloise*, the characters, like those in *Brave New World*, "are constantly made to think they are happy. But they do not *feel* happy."[9] In the *Preface to Narcisse* Rousseau informs us that "in a well constituted state, men are so busy that they have no time for speculation. They are so equal that no one can be preferred as the more learned or shrewd."[10] Finally, in the

Discourse on the Origin of Inequality Among Men, Rousseau en-
dorses the by then traditional Cartesian view that man is fundamentally a machine, a necessary notion for those who would tinker
with the mechanism in order to bring about the really revolutionary revolution.[11]

All of these are important reasons why Rousseau's name should
be invoked in *Brave New World*. But the most important reason
and the real reason, I suspect, why Huxley gives us the clue to
Rousseau is the existence of the Savage. The Savage is, after all,
the incarnation of Rousseau's idea of the noble savage; his appearance in the new world brings about the confrontation of the individual natural man with the artificial society of unnatural men. And
it is precisely because he is noble—a concept utterly foreign to the
inhabitants of the new world—that he becomes the hero, the tragic
hero, of Huxley's novel.[12]

This seems crystal clear, almost self-evident, and yet it is not. By
name he may be savage and by nature noble, a noble Savage, but is
he really a savage, except nominally? And even if savage, does his
nobility arise out of his savagery?

There are some real savages in *Brave New World:* the Pueblo
Indians of Malpais. But these savages appear to be neither noble
nor ignoble; they are merely savage. They do not fit Rousseau's
conception of what primitive men should be like but they do fit
D. H. Lawrence's, whose romanticized view of the Indians Huxley
had attacked as long ago as 1928 in an essay on "The Cold-Blooded
Romantics." "The modern artist," Huxley writes there, "seems to
have grown down; he has reverted to the preoccupations of his
childhood. He is trying to be a primitive. So, it may be remembered, was the romantic Rousseau. But whereas Rousseau's savage
was noble, refined and intelligent, the primitive our modern artists
would like to resemble is a mixture between the Apache and the
fifteen-year-old schoolboy. . . . The ideal life, in their eyes, is one
in which there is plenty of sport, noise, machinery, and sociable
agitation."[13] The Savage contrasts with, rather than shares in, the
savagery of the Pueblo Indians; and his nobility springs less from
his contact with them than from his exclusion from their society.
His nobility is a function of his isolation, of his condition as an
outsider.

In fact, the Savage is no savage at all. Through his extraordinary familiarity with the works of Shakespeare, which he has virtually internalized, the Savage has become a cultivated man. It is he, not Marx or Watson, who is able to engage the only other cultivated person in the novel, Mustapha Mond, on equal, perhaps even superior terms. It is, in fact, the Shakespearean "savage" whom John Savage most closely resembles, someone like the externally unpolished but inwardly highly sensitive Orlando in *As You Like It*.

This is not to say that Huxley does not mean us think of Rousseau in connection with the Savage; he most definitely does. There is even an ironic allusion to Rousseau made by the Savage himself when he attempts to liberate the mob of Delta workers from their subjection to soma—when he tries, as it were, to start a revolution. " 'Don't you want to be free and men? Don't you even understand what mankind and freedom are?' Rage was making him fluent; the words came easily, in a rush. 'Very well, then,' he went on grimly. 'I'll teach you; I'll *make* you be free whether you want to or not' " (174–75). This is an unmistakable allusion to the famous/infamous Rousseauean doctrine that there can be no slaves, not even willing ones, for such perverse creatures would have to be "forced to be free." Ironically, however, the Deltas are too stupid and too numerous to yield either to argument or to force, for they have unwittingly adopted another Rousseauean maxim: they have ceased to be men in order to become perfect citizens.[14]

The Pueblo Indians of Malpais, however, are not the only true savages in *Brave New World*. In a very specific and limited sense, the inhabitants of the new world are also savages. This is a point that Mustapha Mond himself makes while lecturing to students in the garden of the Central London Hatchery and Conditioning Centre. There he connects the old world of intimate family life and vivaporous birth with Freud's analyses of the attendant psychological complexes; but he also makes the connection with "the savages of Samoa" (30) and adds that "in the Trobriands conception was the work of ancestral ghosts; nobody had ever heard of a father" (31). In other words, the savage societies studied by Margaret Mead and Bronislaw Malinowski in the 1920s are among the new world's models of nonrepressive and sexually liberated groups. The new world state, in this sense and in relation to us, is moving not so much into the future as into the past, into the savage past.[15]

By a curious irony, then, it follows that not only the Indian Pueblo but also the new world state is in reality more savage—though not in identical ways—than the Savage himself. Hence the extraordinary man, the cultivated individual, becomes—because he cannot be made to fit in conveniently among either "tribe"—a savage to savages.

Rousseau's relevance to the new world is not exhausted by Huxley's ironic variations on the theme of the noble savage. Rousseau and the whole group of encyclopedic "philosophers" *(philosophes)* to which he partly belonged are among the first and most vociferous prophets of a new god: man. Rousseau functions here as a kind of Prometheus, who frees man from his old bondage to God and Church and sin. "The deepest meaning of Rousseau's thought," according to Ernest Cassirer, "lies in his transposition of the problem of evil from the camp of 'theodicy' into that of 'politics.' The problem of justifying God in the face of the evil of the world, which was so important in the metaphysical religious thought of the 17th and 18th centuries . . . is radically transformed with Rousseau . . . in that the responsibility for the origins of evil is no longer attributed to an obscure wish of God's, or to some presumed original sin by man, but is placed squarely on society." And further: "Rousseau signals a profound and radical transformation of man's whole perspective on his existence. 'Salvation' is no longer entrusted to religion but to politics."[16] In doing so, Rousseau was repeating the Pelagian heresy, which for the young, adamantly Augustinian Huxley was one of the worst blunders a serious thinker could make. Pelagius had denied the existence of original sin; for him Adam's sin stopped with Adam and was not transmitted to Adam's sons and daughters. Man, in other words, was born free even though, as Rousseau put it, he was to be found everywhere in chains. But this was not man's fault; nothing can be man's fault because man is innately good. The fault lies squarely with an abstraction called society, which can be tinkered with or overthrown so as to produce a framework that will allow man to unfold naturally.

For Huxley, the Pelagian heresy was the cornerstone of democratic political theory. Man is free, good, and equal. From Pelagius the road led straight to Rousseau, Helvétius, the French Revolution, and Behaviorist psychology. It was an old dream that modern experience had revealed to be a nightmare. The *philosophes* had

been convinced that man was not only good but that he was growing better all the time, that he was, in fact, perfectible and would
become like unto god. That is why, as Huxley put it in "On the
Charms of History and the Future of the Past" (1927; 1931), "the
future Utopias of Helvétius, Lemercier, and Babeuf, of Godwin
and Shelley, have a certain family resemblance among themselves"
(*Music at Night* 150). They all share a faith in the ideals of democracy and boundless human progress.

In this faith Huxley emphatically does not participate; nor, in his
view, can any truly modern thinker participate in it.

"Nature, we have found," another passage in the same essay
runs, "does rather more, nurture rather less, to make us what we
are than the earlier humanitarians had supposed. We believe in
Mendelian predestination; and in a society not practicing eugenics,
Mendelian predestination leads to pessimism about the temporal
future as Augustinian or Calvinistic predestination leads to pessimism about the eternal future" (157).

The new world state is a fervent practitioner of both eugenics
and of Mendelian predestination.[17] It is, however, also a fervent
adherent of the Pelagian heresy. The two positions are not, in the
final analysis, irreconcilable after all; in the new world state the
dream of the *philosophes* that man can be made perfect has become horribly true, and it has become true precisely because the
new world is superlatively gifted at genetic engineering. Man is
god in the new world; but he is also quite literally god of the
machine, an extraordinarily uninspiring *deus ex machina*.

Rousseau, the *philosophes*, the French Revolution are obviously
not the only political factors lying behind, and contrasting with, the
really revolutionary revolution that has shaped the new world
state. But they are very important factors, and that is why, I think,
Huxley arranges for both Cardinal Newman and Maine de Biran to
put in brief appearances in the novel. These two philosophers
stand in direct opposition to and in reaction against the tradition of
Rousseau and the French Revolution. It is in conversation with the
Savage that Mustapha Mond reads passages from Newman and
Maine de Biran, ostensibly to prove how the new world, by changing the nature of man, has obviated man's need for a god other than
himself. Mond, as the disciple of Rousseau and the *philosophes*, is
satisfied with his proof that the newly constituted man can have no

need for a superhuman god, and, within its limits, his proof is undoubtedly valid. But only within those limits; therein lies the irony that Huxley allows to shine through Mond's certainty. It is only because man has ceased to be fully human and has become a *deus ex machina* that he can abandon God. God is still there; even Mond admits that. It is man who has ceased to exist.

In certain respects the nineteenth-century heirs of Rousseau and the French Revolution are even closer to *Brave New World*. The parable of Henri Saint-Simon, for instance, anticipates the technological emphasis of the new world state, with its contention that only those whose work has a "positive utility" for society are worthy of life. The idea of placing the power of the state entirely in the hands of a scientific elite is also original with Saint-Simon, as is his endowing this elite with the paraphernalia of a priesthood of the "religion of Newton."[18] Eventually this purely scientific religion came to be rejected in favor of a New Christianity in which Saint-Simon became the "scientific pope of humanity and the vicar of God on earth; he made himself out to be the heir of Moses, Socrates, Jesus Christ"—in other words, a kind of Mustapha Mond.[19] In the final version of Saint-Simon's doctrine, the scientists were to share their power with an administrative class and with a new priest class. Mankind was to be divided into three corresponding categories based on an analysis of psychological types: administrators or workers if primarily physical; scientists, if rational; and priests or moralizers, if emotive. With the perfect assignment of each psychological type to his appropriate social function, there would be no possibility for deviation or class conflict. Finally, women were to be emancipated and made equal to men; and this was to be accompanied by a "rehabilitation of the flesh," an aspect of the Saint-Simonian doctrine that was particularly and scandalously stressed by his followers under the leadership of Enfantin.[20]

A sometime disciple of Saint-Simon, Auguste Comte, also elaborated a utopian religion of humanity, again a kind of fusion of scientific or "positivist" and more traditional Christian elements. Thomas Huxley once referred to it as Catholicism without God, a remark Mustapha Mond may be echoing in his description of soma. Unlike Saint-Simon's utopia, however, Comte's was to be virtually sexless. Once the future "subjective synthesis" had been achieved, procreation would be "accomplished by women without the inter-

vention of male bodies, and alimentation [would consist] solely of
liquids and gases. Once men are emancipated from material needs
and desires, time is whiled away in the invention of ever new
expressions of spiritual love; the *gaie science*, Comte calls it."[21]

The most striking anticipation of Huxley's new world state
among these early nineteenth-century utopians is the future society of Charles Fourier. Fourier's phalansteries are as meticulously
planned, economically and psychologically, as the Fordian future.
Each phalanstery would be six stories tall, consisting of a large
central building with two wings. It would be inhabited by exactly
1,620 persons and it would be governed by an elected "Areopa-
gus," which would in turn appoint an executive council. Women
would be emancipated and there would be free love, for Fourier
believed that the Revolution had failed in France because the
family had not been abolished. Hence children would be raised
separately and would amuse themselves chiefly by practicing the
culinary arts and attending the opera. Everyone would be happy,
"because the phalanx would give free and full play to all the passions, life in it would become a series of delights. Its tempo would
accelerate to reach a continuous crescendo. . . . Life itself would
pass as a single moment, as one many-faceted and kaleidoscopic
explosion of rapturous joy." Aside from sexual refinements, there
would also be "gastrosophy," an occupation open to persons of all
ages.[22] "Mondor's Day in Summer"—a supposedly typical day in
Harmony—describes how Mondor rises at 3:30, attends various
meetings, participates in a number of amusements, eats a great
deal, and retires to bed at 10:30.[23] Mond's days at other times of the
year are probably not very different.

All the inhabitants of phalansteries, according to Fourier, will be
psychologically typed and "there would be a sort of card catalogue
where each of the basic 810 types was identified, and if a weary
traveler arrived in a phalanstery he could approach the proper
bureau, be interviewed, have his character determined, and
within a few hours find himself in the presence of a partner with
whom he would be able to establish immediate amorous relations."
Given all this, it is not surprising that "the Fourierist system has
been likened to a bordello where various stimulants are adminis-
tered to provoke capacity for pleasure."[24] It is a political bordello
leading straight to the new world state.

Though less important than Rousseau or the French Revolution and its inheritors for the political structure of the new world state, the Russian Revolution of 1917 also provides a continuous backdrop with which to contrast and complement it.[25] This must be immediately apparent from the names of some of the inhabitants of the new world: Bokanovsky, Lenina, Trotsky, Marx, Engels. It is apparent also from the epigraph to the novel, drawn from the works of one of the subtlest and most impassioned critics of the new Soviet regime, Nicolas Berdyaev. The epigraph speaks in general terms of the modern problem of avoiding utopia now that we are suddenly confronted with the fact that utopia is possible; but the work from which the epigraph is drawn—not named by Huxley—makes it clear that the principal "utopia" that Berdyaev has in mind is that of the Soviet Union. The very title of that work, *The End of Our Time* (1927), is ominous with overtones of the death of an old world and the birthpangs of a new and more horrible one.

Like Newman and Maine de Biran, Berdyaev is convinced that man needs God; and that, paradoxically, it is only possible for God to enter an "imperfect" world. That is why it is futile to attack socialism from a merely bourgeois capitalist perspective. For "socialism is flesh of the flesh and blood of the blood of Capitalism. They both belong to the same world; they are animated by a common spirit—or, rather, by a common negation of spirit."[26] They are both fundamentally atheistic political systems, materialistic creeds dedicated to a purely external progress. What is needed is internal progress, is God.

But socialism is more efficient than capitalism in its atheism. It is in fact a kind of Catholicism without Christianity. "Socialism," according to Berdyaev, "wants in its power the whole of man, soul as well as body, and aims to control over the most intimate places of the spirit. Here is an imitation of the claims of the Christian Church."[27] In Berdyaev's mind socialism is, as it were, by intention at least, the really revolutionary revolution of Huxley's new world state. This is an idea that he derives, consciously I think, from Dostoevski, specifically from the feverish dream of Raskolnikov at the close of *Crime and Punishment*. There socialism is envisioned as a kind of horrible disease, a plague that sweeps all of Europe, killing the souls of its victims.

More than from Berdyaev, however, Huxley got his understanding of Soviet socialism from a remarkable study by René Fuelop-Miller, *The Mind and Face of Bolshevism* (1926), which he first read in 1927. Fuelop-Miller stresses the collectivizing mechanizing aspects of the Russian Revolution, and the consequent destruction of the individual. "While the earlier belief," he writes, "was that the road to salvation, to a higher universal humanity, lay through the perfection of individual personality, Bolshevism has attempted to show that the true path of salvation leads through the annihilation of the individual in a 'mass man' externally organized." We must have heard, Fuelop-Miller continues, the new Bolshevik poets and the "noise orchestral music" of the new musicians, must have seen the new "geometric theatre," and must have participated in the new "joyless joy" of the Bolsheviks "before we can measure the frightful, insanely great sacrifice which Russia has made to an arid idea," to the idea of "a completely lifeless mechanism."[28] This mechanism has become the new Bolshevik religion, with Lenin as its chief prophet and saint: "The 'imitation of the machine' was soon elevated to a religious need, like the 'imitation of Christ' of old; the whole of human society should henceforward be organized on technological priniples." Fuelop-Miller also quotes one of Trotsky's prophetic remarks on what the socialist future will be like: "The socialist mass will rule all nature by the machine. . . . Idealistic blockheads will protest that this is tedious and fruitless—they are indeed blockheads." Here is a dictum worthy of Our Ford himself.[29]

How deep an impression Fuelop-Miller made on Huxley can be gauged from the following passage from "The New Romanticism" (1931): "To the Bolshevik, there is something hideous and unseemly about the spectacle of anything so 'chaotically vital,' so 'mystically organic' as an individual with a soul, with personal tastes, with special talents. Individuals must be organized out of existence; the communist state requires, not men, but cogs and ratchets in the huge 'collective mechanism.' To the Bolshevik idealist Utopia is indistinguishable from one of Mr. Henry Ford's factories. It is not enough, in their eyes, that men should spend only eight hours a day under the workshop discipline. Life outside the factory must be exactly like life inside. Leisure must be as highly organized as toil. Into the Christian Kingdom of Heaven men may only enter if they have become like little children. The condition of entry into the Bolsheviks' Earthly Paradise is that they shall have become like machines" (*Music at Night*, 214).

Huxley goes on, at the end of this passage, to acknowledge his debt specifically to Fuelop-Miller, and then he contrasts this Bolshevik vision of purely collective man with that of the purely individual ideal of the equally atheistic democratic romantics. "The political doctrines elaborated by Lenin and his followers," Huxley writes, "are the exact antithesis to the revolutionary liberalism preached by Godwin and dithyrhambically chanted by Shelley a hundred years ago. Godwin and Shelley believed in pure individualism. The Bolsheviks believe in pure collectivism. One belief is as extravagantly romantic as the other" (215). Applied to *Brave New World*, as Huxley obviously did apply it, this conclusion explains why Huxley condemns both the collectivized mechanical men of the new world state—because he out-bolsheviks even the Bolsheviks—and the pure individual in the person of the Savage— because, as the Savage's tragic fate demonstrates, man is more (and also less) than a pure individual.

From Fuelop-Miller and, to a lesser degree, from Berdyaev, Huxley transported into his new world the idea of a totally planned, godless society. In doing so, however, Huxley appears to fall into an inconsistency. Mond, after all, tells the Savage that his world has abolished the need for God, yet one of the most effective scenes of the novel shows Bernard Marx taking part in a religious ceremony: the Solidarity Service, at the orgiastic conclusion of which it seems as if a kind of black Holy Ghost descends upon the supine participants. The presence in the novel of an Arch-Songster, an archbishop of sorts, also suggests that the new world state places an official value on religion.

These are obvious contradictions, but only, I think, superficially so. The Solidarity Service has all the external trappings of a religious ceremony, a kind of combination of Christian revivalism and a Dionysiac rite. But the "Greater Being" who is addressed and summoned in the service is not really Our Ford, even though the worshipers seem to hear his footsteps at the door; the greater being is the worshipers themselves, who fuse in "atonement and final consummation of solidarity, the coming of the Twelve-in-One, the incarnation of the Greater Being" (70). The Solidarity Service is just what it says it is; a service of solidarity and even of identity:

"For I am you and you are I," as the Third Solidarity Hymn has it
(68). The Solidarity Service is not a religious service; it is the
substitute for a religious service, just as the Arch-Songster is the
substitute for an archbishop. The Solidarity Service satisfies the
religious feeling; it does not serve God. It bears the same relation
to God as the Violent Passion Surrogate bears to passion. Man,
even new world man, retains the need occasionally to feel passion-
ately or religiously, and such feelings must be gratified. But this
has nothing to do with real religion or real passion.[30]

There are precedents for this, as Huxley very well knew. The
French Revolution had its Feast of Reason and worshiped the
rational goddess in the Cathedral of Notre Dame. The Russian
Revolution has its May Day and, as both Berdyaev and Fuelop-
Miller contend, is in itself a kind of secular substitute for religion.

There is also another and final connection between the Soviet
Revolution and the new world, one that derives from yet another
attack inspired by and directed against that revolution: a novel,
Three Pairs of Silk Stockings and a collection of short stories, *Without Cherry Blossom*, both by Panteleimon Romanof. Of Romanof's
novel Huxley wrote to his father in August 1931 that "it's much the
most real and convincing account of life in Russia—particularly life
for the intellectual class—I have ever read" (L,352). The short
stories Huxley cites in his essay, "Obstacle Race" (1931), as examples of "moral flat racing" or unrestrained promiscuity. "The flattest
racing in the world," Huxley concluded, "at any rate in the sphere
of sexual relationships, is modern Russian racing." This conclusion
is supported by a quotation from Romanof's title story, in which a
young woman student confesses that "for us love does not exist; we
have only sexual relationships."[31] This new laxity relative to the old
Victorian code of sexual mores was, of course, by no means
confined to the Soviet Union. Huxley's novels of the twenties describe the same phenomenon in detail and with relish in a British
context; and he had seen it in full flower in Southern California,
while returning from his extended tour of the Far East, so that the
new world state's ethic of promiscuity is hardly to be laid entirely
at the door of the Soviet Union. While this is true, there is still a
difference between Soviet sexuality—as described, say, in
Romanof—and the Western postwar casual attitude toward sex.
The former was an official attitude of the state—an attitude that

was, by the way, also officially changed soon thereafter; the latter was a spontaneous shift in cultural and personal values which, if anything, was opposed by the state. The essential difference may be appreciated in an observation like the following from Bertrand Russell's *Marriage and Morals* (1929): "There is no country in the world and there has been no age in the world's history where sexual ethics and sexual institutions have been determined by rational considerations, with the exception of Soviet Russia."[32]

This new rational sexual ethic of the Soviets, as depicted in Romanof's fiction, comes remarkably close to the new world ethic of promiscuity. In Romanof's Soviet Union, as in Huxley's new world, those who seek love rather than merely sex are laughed at. "The girls live with their men friends," the passage quoted by Huxley from Romanof goes on to say, "and it is a small matter to go with them for a week or a month, or promiscuously, for one night only. And anyone who is trying to find in love anything beyond the physiological is laughed down as mental or a bad case."[33] The problem of a modern virtuous young woman—Vera's problem in Romanof's story, "The Right to Love"—is no longer the traditional problem of how to retain her virtue, but rather of how to lose it. Sexual virtue, in the Soviet Union as in the new world, has become a sin, or even worse, a ridiculous absurdity. Helmholtz Watson's incredulous laughter at Romeo's exclusive passion for Juliet would almost be as appropriate in the Soviet context.

It is also because of Romanof, I think, that Huxley chooses to give his heroine the name Lenina. She is the embodiment of Romanof's Soviet woman, dutiful in a promiscuity that in reality is not natural to her. It is even possible that Huxley may have been directly inspired to create Lenina by a character named Lena in another one of the stories in *Without Cherry Blossom*. This story, "Her Condition," recounts how Lena, a properly promiscuous good-timer, is pursued, even hounded by an uncouth and old-fashioned suitor, who loves her and does not merely desire her. Victor, the frustrated lover, grows more and more savage at her ridicule and rejection of his sincere attentions, until one day he tries to kill her. He almost succeeds, and the result of his savagery is that suddenly Lena returns his love and abandons her earlier promiscuous life and friends.

The outcome and the externals of this story are, of course, very different from the story of Lenina and the Savage. But there is an essential similarity between them: like Lena, Lenina is at first unable to comprehend what it is that the Savage wants from her, for she can only think of love in physiological terms; but like Lena, though more slowly and much less consciously, Lenina becomes dimly aware of a force other and more powerful than sex: love. And it is the savagery of the Savage, his ability to hurt her and even his threat to kill her, that help to bring about this change, just as Victor's savage passion does with Lena.

The Russian Revolution, with all its attendant social and cultural phenomena, exercises a profound influence on the shape of Huxley's new world state, almost as profound as that of the French Revolution. Despite the manifold ways in which both of these revolutions anticipate the really revolutionary revolution, however, they are ultimately only external or "unreal" revolutions; they do not finally attempt to change the essential inner characteristics of humanity but assume that outward changes in political and social structure are sufficient to ensure stability. This stress on political, economic, and social egalitarianism is something that both of these revolutions share also with the third great political revolution of modern times, the American Revolution. Huxley's personal experience of the effects of this revolution, during his visit to the United States in 1926, was, as we have seen, to leave a powerful imprint on *Brave New World*. But there is also a less personal and more theoretical connection between the French Revolution, the American Revolution, and the new world state, a connection that was made for Huxley by another and earlier visitor to the United States, Alexis de Tocqueville.

Tocqueville, like Maine de Biran, was one of the great nineteenth-century thinkers in reaction against Rousseau and the Revolution of 1789. He dreaded the consequences of rampant egalitarianism and saw in the United States, for all its admirable qualities, an example of what the future would bring to the rest of the world. The passion for equality, he noted, tended to outweigh and perhaps even exclude the love for liberty; and, even worse, it tended also to level downward and destroy all desirable variety in an effort to standardize and equalize mankind. "It is believed by some," he writes in *Democracy in America*, "that modern society will be ever changing its aspect; for myself, I fear that it will ultimately be too invariably fixed in the same institutions, the same prejudices, the same manners, so that mankind will be stopped and circumscribed; that the mind will swing backwards and forwards forever, without begetting fresh ideas; that man will waste his strength in bootless and solitary trifling; and, though in continual motion, that humanity will cease to advance."[34]

Basing his conclusions on his study of the democratic institutions and inhabitants of the United States, as well as his knowledge of the developments of the French Revolution and its origins in Rousseau and the *philosophes*, Tocqueville ventured to predict near the close of *Democracy in America* what he thought the future political and social conditions of life would be like. This prediction, more than that of any other single political thinker, comes closest to outlining the structure of Huxley's new world state and is therefore worth quoting here with only slight omissions: "I think then that the species of oppression by which democratic nations are menaced is unlike anything which has ever before existed in the world: our contemporaries will find no prototype of it in their memories. . . . The first thing that strikes the observation is an innumerable multitude of men all equal and alike, incessantly endeavouring to procure the petty and paltry pleasures with which they glut their lives. . . . Above this race of men stands an immense and tutelary power, which takes upon itself alone to procure their gratifications, and to watch over their fate. That power is absolute, minute, regular, provident, and mild. It would be like the authority of a parent, if, like that authority, its object was to prepare men for manhood; but it seeks on the contrary to keep them in perpetual childhood: it is well content that the people should rejoice, provided they think of nothing but rejoicing. For their happiness such a government willingly labors, but it chooses to be the sole agent and only arbiter of that happiness: it provides for their security, foresees and supplies their necessities, facilitates their pleasures, manages their principal concerns, directs their industry, regulates the descent of property, and subdivides their inheritances—what remains, but to spare them all the care of thinking and the trouble of living? . . . The will of man is not shattered, but softened, bent, and guided: men are seldom forced by it to act, but they are constantly restrained from acting; such a power does not destroy, but it prevents existence; it does not tyrannize, but it compresses, enervates, extinguishes, and stupefies a people, till each nation is reduced to be nothing better than a flock of kind and industrious animals, of which the government is the shepherd."[35]

The immense and mild tutelary power of Tocqueville's vision of the future—a power strongly reminiscent of Rousseau's legislator—becomes in Huxley's novel the mild and immensely powerful Mustapha Mond. Like the tutelary power, Mond is a "good" shepherd who does everything for his charges as long as they remain sheep, as long as they "glut their lives" with insignificant pleasures and devote themselves entirely to an infantile and meaningless happiness.

For Tocqueville, this future horror will be the result of the present insistence on egalitarian democracy. With Huxley, as we have seen, there are also other important factors, but certainly strict egalitarianism plays a role, especially egalitarianism of the American variety. The United States, for Huxley, represented a fusion of some of the worst features of the Rousseauean ideal of democratic political equality and Soviet mechanization. "The democratic hypothesis in its extreme and most popular form," Huxley wrote in the American section of his travelogue, *Jesting Pilate* (1926), "is that all men are equal and that I am just as good as you are. It is so manifestly untrue that a most elaborate system of humbug has had to be invented to render it credible to any normally sane human being. Nowhere has this system of humbug been brought to such perfection as in America" (276). The result of such humbug, however, is that it becomes impossible to survive in this society unless, as Huxley notes in *Do What You Will* (1929), one is a mere "cog" like Babbitt or an efficient and inhuman organizer like Ford. If one wishes to live fully and harmoniously as, for example, Blake or Burns did, then one is "doomed to almost certain social disaster" (36). For the same reason, in the new world state the Savage is also doomed to disaster. The problem is that the new world state, like America, is a plutocracy, and in a plutocracy "the world of Pericles and Lorenzo the Magnificent becomes the world of Hoover and Ford" (29). Significantly, there are no aristocratic names whatever in the new world state; aristocracy is prohibited there and in America alike.

It is precisely this system of exclusion of anyone who either does not possess money-brains, like Ford, or who works in behalf of money-brains, like Babbitt, that Huxley calls Fordism. Fordism is an ascetic religion that worships the deities of cash and efficiency and that "demands the cruellest mutilations of the human psyche" in order to placate those gods" (*Music at Night*, 180). Ford's aim is to make the world over into a single great factory, run according to the most orthodox principles of Taylorized efficiency.

Huxley was by no means alone in noting the ominous effects of Fordism on modern life. Ford's enormous success as a car manu- facturer, coupled with his vociferous anti-intellectualism and ap- parent contempt for anything but profits and efficiency, evoked a multitude of hostile literary responses in the 1920s and 1930s. Though it is difficult to say with any certainty which of these attacks Huxley may have read, he can hardly have escaped them all. Let me quote from a selection of these works, all of them antedating *Brave New World*. "To the observant European," writes Colonel J. F. C. Fuller in *Atlantis, Or America and the Future* (1926), "the American is little more than human coal. To obtain the utmost efficiency out of this fuel, work is standardized, in order to obtain a higher output in a given time. Economically, this may be profitable, but not only is the Ford car produced in its millions, but also the Ford mind."[36] Garet Garrett's *Ouroboros, Or the Me- chanical Extension of Mankind* (1925), sees Ford's method of financing his sales through credit as destroying the old virtue of thrift for the sake of the new virtue of consumerism: "To con- sume—to consume more and more progressively—to be able to say in the evening 'I have consumed more to-day than I consumed yesterday,' this now is the duty the individual owes to industrial society."[37] André Siegfried, in *America Comes of Age* (1927, French; 1928, English), sees that "prince of industrial output," Henry Ford, as responsible for turning millions of American work- men into automatons: "'Fordism,' which is the essence of Ameri- can industry, results in the standardization of the workman himself. Artisanship, now out of date, has no place in the New World, but with it have disappeared certain conceptions of man- kind which we in Europe consider the very basis of civilization."[38] According to R. M. Fox's *The Triumphant Machine* (1928), "Ford stands for the industrial magnate view of life. To him the mass of men must be definitely subordinate to things. They are of use only in making things. His own reason for being in the world is to produce cheap motor cars." Since, however, it is impossible for him to occupy all of his time in this task—or in hobbies like restoring furniture or houses—"he cannot conceal his boredom. In his scheme of life there is no apparent place for books, music, pictures, art. Where Mr. Ford handles cultural problems he is like a naked savage with a pair of trousers—he keeps them folded, creased, brushed, but he is not quite sure where they belong. Art has no essential place in his scheme of life. . . . "[39] S. D. Schmalhausen argues in *Behold America* (1931) that "America's greatest men are almost without exception cultural dumbbells, intellectual and emotional morons. . . . To study this remarkable defective [Henry Ford] is to appreciate everything that is inadequate and inoffensive and emotionally obtuse in our extroverted land. . . . The intellectual and emotional blind spots that account for the anemic state of our culture are nowhere more disastrously in evidence than in the drawfish mind and constricted heart of that greatest bourgeois of them all, Henry Ford, the Mussolini of American business."[40]

Then, of course, there is Ford himself, either in his "own" writings or as quoted by others. Ford's principal literary achievement, *My Life and Work* (1922), is a fascinating account of his devotion to the assembly line; this is also the work that, in the new world state, has replaced the Bible, bound as it is "in limp black leather-surrogate and stamped with large golden Ts" (171). Though mostly a straightforward history of Ford's life in overcoming manifold obstacles in the way of salvation by mass-production, it occasionally rises to more "philosophical" levels, as in the following passage: "We speak of creative 'artists' in music, painting, and the other arts. We seemingly limit the creative functions to productions that may be hung on gallery walls, or played in concert halls, or otherwise displayed where idle and fastidious people gather to admire each other's culture. But if a man wants a field for vital creative work, let him come where he is dealing with higher laws than those of sound, or line, or color; let him come where he may deal with the laws of personality. We want artists in industrial relationship. We want masters in industrial method—both from the standpoint of the product and the producer. We want those who can mould the political, social, industrial, and moral mass into a sound and shapely whole."[41] In practical terms, however, the answer to this lyrical cry for industrial artistry turns out, on the evidence of *My*

Life and Work, to be quite prosaic. Experts, for example, are definitely not wanted, for "we have most unfortunately found it necessary to get rid of a man as soon as he thinks himself an expert—because no one ever considers himself expert if he really knows his job." The only expert, in other words, and the final arbiter of industrial artistry, is Henry Ford himself. His sound and shapely work-force consists of multiples of a kind of worker who does not wish to exert himself and who, above all, "wants a job in which he does not have to think." This sort of a job Ford is delighted to be able to provide, for though he confesses that he does not like such jobs himself, he has "not been able to discover that repetitive labour injures a man in any way."[42]

In a later work, *My Philosophy of Industry* (1929), Ford delivers himself of a series of paeans to the machine, the factory, and the consumer-oriented business economy. If we will but consign ourselves body and soul to the machine, then the promised land of Coca-Cola and Ford cars will be ours to enter, for "machinery is accomplishing in the world what man has failed to do by preaching, propaganda, or the written word."[43] Because of machines and big business, a time is coming, according to Ford, when people will be able to "retain their health, vitality, and mental keenness for many years longer." And if not, why there is no real problem, because the human machine can be fixed just like any other machine: "There is every reason to believe that we should be able to renew our human bodies in the same manner as we renew [sic] a defect in a boiler." The highway to utopia lies open before us, ready to be traveled down in the comfort of a Ford car, consuming ever more and ever more quickly as we drive along. "Human demands are increasing every day," the Detroit oracle of consumerism informs us, "and the needs for the gratification are increasing also. This is as it should be. Gradually, under the benign influence of American industry, wives are released from work, little children are no longer exploited; and, given more time, they both become free to go out and find new products, new merchants and manufacturers who are supplying them. Thus business grows."[44]

Though Ford sought (unsuccessfully) to make use of the democratic process as a means for getting his ideas, and his person, into political power, he was staunchly opposed to the idea of democracy itself. "Business holds no place for democracy," he proclaims in

Moving Forward (1930), "if by democracy is meant the shaping of politics by the vote for a large number of people or their delegates. The theory of democratic government as applied to a nation has never proved sufficiently practical even to be tried. This is because the theory makes no provision at all for getting anything done. It starts and it stops with discussion." Like Wells, Ford was for replacing the politician with the practical businessman and the engineer. "Substituting the engineer for the politician," he writes in the same work, "is a very natural step forward." And further: "Engineering spells freedom. Men were held to a single spot before the engineer came. By steam and motor car and airplane he has liberated man."[45]

In the twenties the New York-based League-For-A-Living attempted to systematize Ford's thinking and to put it across as a panacea for America's ills. One of the League's pamphlets, *365 of Henry Ford's Sayings*, culled from Ford's publications and from his conversation, makes Ford seem like a combination of Jesus Christ and Benjamin Franklin, the subject at once of a gospel and a kind of Rich Henry's Almanac. The pamphlet's afterword poses the question as to whether "'the Ford principle,' which he has demonstrated so successfully in his private business [can] be applied to the nation's affairs." The triumphant answer is, not unexpectedly, that it can. "Henry Ford could do it. He could organize such a national system. He possesses in himself the power of expert Leadership adequate to bringing about an economic revolution which would open a new era of peace and plenty."[46] This change, however, would come about through economic evolution, not political revolution.

Not only is history "bunk" for Ford, but painting, sculpture, music, and all culture are "bunk." "I don't like to read books," Ford confesses; "they mess up my mind."[47] What is not bunk, however, is machine-culture, is "the motion-picture with its universal language, the airplane with its speed, and the radio with its coming international program." These are not bunk because they "will soon bring the whole world to complete understanding. Thus may we envision a United States of the World. Ultimately it will surely come." But we must work for this vision to be realized, for "work does more than get us our living: it gets us our life."[48] Not any work, however, will do the trick; it must be work conducted according to the latest principles of efficiency.

The greatest modern prophet of efficiency was Frederick Winslow Taylor, whose *Principles of Scientific Management* (1911) Henry Ford swore by. Taylor was the first man to break a job down into its constituent movements, come up with an "ideal" time within which each movement was to be carried out, and then relate the whole job to a particular type of worker. One of Taylor's great triumphs was the rationalization of the pig-iron industry. His conclusion was that "one of the very first requirements for a man who is fit to handle pig iron as a regular occupation is that he shall be so stupid and so phlegmatic that he more nearly resembles in his mental make-up the ox than any other type. The man who is mentally alert and intelligent is for this very reason entirely unsuited to what would, for him, be the grinding monotony of work of this character. Therefore the workman who is best suited to handling pig iron is unable to understand the real science of doing this class of work."[49] Even better suited than the human ox was the gorilla, and, indeed, Taylor quite seriously maintained that "this work is so crude and elementary in its nature that the writer firmly believes that it would be possible to train an intelligent [*sic*] gorilla so as to become a more efficient pig-iron handler than any man can be." Payment for work completed by such gorillas, animal or human, must also be nicely and "scientifically" calculated; bonuses, for instance, should never exceed sixty percent of base, lest the workers grow shiftless. Moreover, rewards "to be effective in stimulating men to do their best work, must come soon after the work has been done," for most men are unable to think or to plan for more than a very short period beyond the present moment.[50] Taylorism, it should be clear by now, bears the same relationship to society as behaviorism bears to the individual, and both of these new "sciences" are, characteristically, American.

In the United States, during the first decades of this century, a craze for efficiency swept through much of the population. The engineer and the technocrat (embodied in someone like Hoover) became the new ideal human types; and the principles of efficient factory management were to be applied to the home and even to the church. The Reverend Charles Stelzle, author of *The Princi-*

ples of Successful Church Advertizing, is an example of the sort of person who wished to make religion efficient.[51]

Anyone who has bothered to read Ford and Taylor, along with their many imitators and critics, can quickly appreciate why Huxley begins his description of the new world state with a factory organized according to Taylor's principles of scientific management. This is not a Ford factory producing automobiles, but it is a factory producing human beings as if they were Ford automobiles. Just as in the Ford factory, each step in production is carefully timed and each task is assigned to just the right kind of worker.[52] The whole operation is supervised by men like Henry Foster and the DHC, people dedicated to the cult of statistics and efficiency. Their minds—like Ford's and Taylor's—are completely taken up (and in) by the task, with no room left over to inquire what the point of the task might be.

Huxley's Deltas and Epsilons are the equivalents of Taylor's gorillas and human oxen. They are deliberately bred to be just intelligent enough to do the job they are predestined for, and to be too stupid to understand or want to understand anything else. So too the soma distribution, which is interrupted by the Savage, is conducted entirely according to Taylor's principle of reward following quickly on the completion of work. In fact, everything in the new world state has been Taylorized; it is the efficiency craze carried to its craziest and most logical extreme.

The factory for human beings, with which Huxley's novel begins, is the symbol of the political structure of the new world state. In the Fordian future, the whole world has become a factory: the lives of the human products are planned minutely to the last detail. Their roles in society are predestined, their thoughts are predestined, their leisure-time activities are predestined, even the length of time during which their bodies will function is predestined. Their development can be measured, as it were, by their stations in the assembly line of life.

That Huxley—along with Ford's other critics—is to some degree distorting Ford's views and achievements for satirical purposes is of course quite clear. Though culturally Ford was undoubtedly a boor, he had a good, commonsensical intelligence that was very much his own. A book like *Ford Ideals* (1922), which is made up of selections from "The Dearborn Independent," contains sentiments often remarkably like those Huxley himself was propagating: for the thoughtful use of natural resources (including what we nowadays call re-cycling) and against the exploitation of poorer nations by the richer; for craftsmanship and against the dehumanizing impersonality of the modern factory system; for the preservation of old customs and monuments and against the unlimited cancerous growth of modern cities; for a fair and equal distribution of wealth and against the brutalizing doctrine of success. That he knew that he was turning into something like Our Ford in the eyes of Europeans especially is apparent from his remarks about the alleged Americanization of Europe in *Moving Forward*. The United States, Ford maintains, is not responsible for turning Europe into a factory; Europe had already been a factory for generations, but an unprosperous and poorly managed factory. And "as to the fear of what is called 'American standardization,' I quite understand it; we should all fear it if it were anything like the notion of it which haunts the European mind. It is doubtful if the European who visits America ever sees the thing that he fears. It is not life that is standardized; it is rather that the standards of the goods and the services that minister to life have been raised to a higher level than formerly. If American standardization meant that everything was to be cut to the same pattern, it would have destroyed itself long ago."[53]

Ford, however, was quite wrong in implying that fear of "Americanization" was limited to Europeans like Huxley. In *Man and Machines* (1929), Stuart Chase focuses on a number of the same elements in American culture that were to strike Huxley as ominous: Ford, of course, and Taylor, but also Alexander Graham Bell's desire to produce a "smello-meter"; also the deadening dullness of the American way of life, as exemplified by the Lynds's study of Middletown; also the teaching of foreign languages by hypnopaedia; also the utter vacuity of American amusements, with Sunday drives "past Goodrich Tire Signs and Travelers' Rests," or with millions "seated in the dark watching a personable young woman alternately mislay and recover her virtue for six thick rolls of celluloid"; also the churches, which engage in advertising, just like any other big business; also the almost cancerous mania for consumption. Like Huxley, Chase foresees an end to modern life in a "Two Hour War" in which airplanes destroy the world's cities, a disaster that leads to a capitalist seizure of power, with a Bellamy-like supertrust running the government "for a flat eight percent on its own new issues."[54]

Ralph Borsodi's *This Ugly Civilization* (1929) also generalizes and extrapolates on the American experience. Again Ford and Taylor are in the forefront. They are chiefly responsible for the system of serial production, in which production itself becomes its own end. This new system of production also has the effect of providing increased leisure time for the work force, and hence new amusements have to be devised to "kill" this leisure time. Borsodi suggests that in the "industrial utopia" of the future the weary urbanite will be "whisked away in an aerial taxi to the great Hotel Avoirdupois at the top of one of the peaks in the Catskills—the resort that he has selected for his weekend. He will register at the office and be assigned a number, a room, a table, and a food-class. . . . Then he will begin a six-day eating marathon of, perhaps, twelve meals per day. Between meals he will of course visit the great eliminatories which will be the real pride of the Hotel Avoirdupois. All the appliance of science, manipulated by skilled physicians, nurses, and masseurs, will make it possible for him to return to the table with every bit of his previous meal completely eliminated from his system. . . . At the end of the six days, he will check out of the resort in perfect condition and return to work having had a most enjoyable week-end."[55]

Huxley's games of Centrifugal Bumblepuppy and Obstacle Golf, his jazz by the Sixteen Sexophonists, his feelies, soma holidays, and escalator squash are less gastronomical than Borsodi's Hotel Avoirdupois, but their purpose is the same: to increase consumption—of transport or manufactured equipment—to kill time and to avoid the possibility of ever being alone. Such distractions are ways of spending time in decreation, rather than recreation.

Serial production in the factory has also divided the world, according to Borsodi, into two classes: the managers and the "cogs," just as it has in Huxley's world. These cogs are, like the products of those factories, standardized, and they are all standardized downward, because "the factory system involves an apotheosis of the mediocre. The least common denominator of taste is made the standard to which, on the score of efficiency, everything must conform." The factory system has also helped to destroy the home and the family. The new-style home has become the apartment hotel because it "best meets the needs of a factory economy." When the whole population is housed in such apartment hotels, then alienation and standardization will be complete. This future population, however, will not include old people, because the factory system has no use for them: "For youth, the school. For maturity, the factory, For old age, nothing."[56]

Even more strongly than Chase or Borsodi, Georges Duhamel attacks the American way of life in *America the Menace, Scenes from the Life of the Future* (1930, French; 1931, English). Americans, according to Duhamel, are the willing and eager slaves of the entertainment industry, obedient to the law that "the citizen must not be bored; that is, he must not be roused from his bovine torpor." Everything, including human beings and even the legs of American women, are mass-produced and standardized. Mass spectacle sport has taken the place of religion, to the immense profit of the organizing entrepreneurs. The individual has vanished. More than any other country in the West, the United States approximates Maeterlinck's vision, in *The Life of the Bee* (1901), of an insect society. "If steel machinery refuses to make profitable progress," Duhamel remarks ironically, "nothing remains except to turn to man, and modify the human machine. Breed, O America, the human tool. . . . Can you not engage in scientific human breeding and selection? Since you have already subjected certain specimens of humanity to sterilization, is it impossible for you to imitate the bees and the ants, and create a body of people, sexless, devoid of passion, exclusively devoted to the instruction, the feeding, and the defense of the city?"[57]

Modern Europe, Duhamel concludes, is faced with the choice of moving in one of two directions: that of America or that of the Soviet Union. But the Russian alternative is one that is entirely political and ideological, and therefore ultimately superficial. America, on the other hand, represents a future that is beyond mere politics and ideology; it involves a change in humanity and not just in government.[58]

In this conclusion Duhamel comes close to seeing in the United States what Huxley calls the really revolutionary revolution. And it certainly seems true that for Huxley also the United States, more than the French Revolution or the Soviet Union, was the harbinger of the final and most profound revolution. Ford, not Rousseau or Lenin, is explicitly recognized as the founder and inspiration—the "god"—of the new world state.

It is also from Ford and from industrialized America, as well as to some degree from Mussolini's fascism, that the new world state derives its caste system. Democratic egalitarianism is, after all, only "humbug" in the United States; the reality of inequality is disguised by this humbug, but it cannot be abolished. The entire factory system is built on the assumption of inequality, on the existence of three distinct classes: the tiny class of entrepreneurs like Ford; the somewhat larger but still relatively small class of managers; and the vast class of workers. This is also roughly the nature and the ratio of the castes in the new world state, with the Controllers at the top, the Alphas managing the day-to-day affairs of the factory/state, and the other castes from Beta to Epsilon doing the more or less routine chores.

A caste system, to be sure, is different from a class system. A class system allows for the possibility of class conflict, because of the differing interests of the various classes. A caste system— evocative of such traditionally stable societies as China and India— obviates such conflict because each caste is genetically and socially conditioned to function without conflict. The Alpha caste, from which also the Controllers are drawn, is genetically an exception to this rule, but not socially; nonconforming Alphas are simply removed from the society before they can endanger it, as happens with Bernard Marx and Helmholtz Watson.

The existence of a caste system in the new world is, however, in a sense puzzling. Other creators of future states—Wells, for instance, or Forster in "The Machine Stops"—had foreseen a time when man would liberate himself from the need to do any kind of manual labor whatever: machines would take care of all that for him. Why Huxley did not choose to provide his new world state with machine slaves instead of human ones is not entirely clear. He had certainly read both Wells and Forster, and he probably knew more about modern technology and its potential for the future than both of those writers put together. He must have known, at any rate, that technologically speaking there was no reason why nearly all of the work done in the new world state by Epsilons, Deltas, Gammas, and even Betas could not be carried out equally well and more cheaply by machines. But while the new world state possesses very sophisticated machines of all sorts—games, vehicles, TV, "feelies," and so on—there seem to be none of the expected labor-saving devices. Even the elevator in the Central London Hatchery and Conditioning Centre requires an Epsilon Minus attendant to run it.[59]

Why is this so? The answer to this question lies, I think, in Huxley's perception that a truly stable state demands superiority and inferiority. "The optimum population," as Mustapha Mond tells the Savage, "is modelled on the iceberg—eight-ninths below the water line, one-ninth above" (183). And he tells him too that the Inventions Office is stuffed full with thousands of labor-saving devices, none of which the Controllers propose to put to use. Hence if there are Epsilon workers rather than machines in the new world state, there are very good psychosocial reasons for their presence.

The real reason for the existence of castes is that only in a society stratified according to ability is it possible (1) to satisfy the basic human desire (and need) to feel superior to someone else; and (2) to avoid an internecine struggle for power, resulting from an inability to express one's superiority in socially accepted ways. Therefore the feeling of superiority has been institutionalized in the new world state. "I'm glad I'm not a Gamma" (52), Lenina tells Henry Foster, repeating what is obviously part of a hypnopaedic lesson from her infancy. Later she ventures to suppose that "Epsilons don't really mind being Epsilons," and receives from Henry the reply that "'of course they don't. How can they? They don't know what it's like being anybody else. We'd mind of course. But then we've been differently conditioned. Besides, we start with a different heredity.' 'I'm glad I'm not an Epsilon,' said Lenina with conviction. 'And if you were an Epsilon,' said Henry, 'your conditioning would have made you no less thankful that you weren't a Beta or an Alpha.'" (62).

As an Alpha, and especially as an Alpha whose work consists of supervising the process of conditioning, Henry is able to understand something of the effects of trained responses. This is also true of Bernard Marx, but because of his stunted, non-Alpha physique Bernard has abnormal difficulty expressing his superiority. Bernard envies other Alphas like Henry and Benito Hoover, who are able to take their superiority for granted and who move "through the caste system as a fish through water—so utterly at home as to be unaware either of themselves or of the beneficent and comfortable element in which they had their being" (54). Bernard's inability to carry off his superiority is a cautionary example of what happens when the innate feelings of social superiority are frustrated.

That Epsilons who are at the bottom of the human scale are unable to feel superior to any other caste does not really matter. As Henry points out, they are conditioned to sense their inferiority as a kind of superiority; and, in any case, their abysmally low level of intelligence does not permit them to feel or perceive anything but the most elementary human wants. It is significant, however, that the new world state seems to have perpetuated the traditional system of sex role inequality. On the evidence provided, at any rate, Alpha males tend to seek the company of Beta females; the only exception to this rule is the Bernard Marx/Miss Keate affair. In this respect too, then, feelings of inequality seem generally to be reinforced.

Inequality is very consciously built into the structure of the new world state, partly because the model of Ford's factory demands it but principally because Huxley's conception of human nature also requires it. That is why Huxley contends that "contemporary prophets [including, obviously, himself] have visions founded on the idea of natural inequality, not of natural equality . . . of a ruling aristocracy slowly improved . . . by deliberate eugenic breeding" (*Music at Night*, 152). And that is why "we can imagine our children having visions of a new caste system based on differences of native ability and accompanied by a Machiavellian system of education, designed to give the members of the lower castes only such education as it is profitable for society at large and the upper castes in particular that they should have." Here in a nutshell is the rationale for the caste system of the new world state.

At the very top of the iceberg of inequality sits Mustapha Mond, along with nine other World Controllers. Just how the institution of World Controllership was originally established, the novel does not tell us, but it is clear, from what we know of the history of Mustapha Mond, that the institution is self-perpetuating and self-selective. In this it resembles contemporary institutions like the

Soviet Comintern, or older ones like the ruling Cardinals of the Church, or (Huxley's most likely immediate model) Plato's philosopher king. We know that Mond was selected and even to some unknown extent trained for his position of authority; and we know too that he both reads philosophy (William James, Maine de Biran, Newman) and philosophizes himself. Like Plato's royal philosopher, Mond's philosophy has only one aim: to preserve the stability and happiness of the state. To achieve this end all means are permissible, as far as both Mond and Plato are concerned: racism and political inequality (the infamous Myth of the Metals in *The Republic*); propaganda or the right of the philosopher king to lie to his people for their own benefit; abomination of culture and the arts; eugenics, or the breeding of men and women from identical castes so as to perpetuate those castes; and even free sex, at least for soldiers during times of war.

The chief difference between Plato's philosopher king and Huxley's world controller seems to be that the latter is able to exercise his authority with much greater flexibility. We are told, in the course of the novel, of two vast social experiments conducted by the World Controllers: one in Cyprus, when twenty-two thousand Alphas were allowed to manage their own society; and the other in Ireland, when the experiment of drastically reducing the normal work load was attempted. Both experiments ended in failure, but the very fact that they were undertaken at all reveals an openness of mind and a relative readiness to entertain social novelties that are quite uncharacteristic of the ruler of Plato's republic. Indeed, the very fact that the Savage is permitted to enter the new world state is the result of Mond's desire to conduct an "experiment," to see what will happen when a natural man enters an utterly unnatural environment. Rather than allow the Savage to return to the Reservation or to send him into exile with Marx and Watson, Mond is also determined to see his experiment out to the bitter end.

The new world state, then, is very definitely a political entity, even though in it political responsibility ultimately rests in the hands of a very few rulers. The politics of this state consists precisely in depriving all other citizens of the ability and even the desire to exercise anything like political rights; the notion of "right" is in any case utterly alien to the anti-individualistic new world state. When political acts are committed by those who are not authorized to do so, as when the Savage and Helmholtz Watson disturb the soma distribution, then such acts are treated as crimes and punished by exile. The ideal of political power in the new world state, however, is to be as nearly invisible as possible. The state, when functioning as it should, runs itself, without any interference from above. It functions entirely according to the Marxist golden rule of from each according to his ability and to each according to his need, with the proviso that no one can possess an ability or feel a need that has not been previously engineered into the system. It is only on this condition that the state seems, as it were, to wither away and the gates to "paradise" are once again thrown open.

5

Conclusion:
The Two Futures: A.F. 632 and 1984

Aldous Huxley is the most shattering satirist in English since Swift.

> A. C. Ward, *The Nineteen-Twenties*

BRAVE New World is by far Huxley's most popular book, though it probably is not, as A. E. Dyson once remarked, his best book.[1] Huxley's mind was too wide-ranging and his art too complex to be fully contained in a short satirical novel like this one; to really appreciate what Huxley can do in the novel one has to turn to the bigger, more comprehensive, and more ambitious works like *Eyeless in Gaza* and *Point Counter Point*. As Huxley himself argued, the final standard of a work of art is its approximation to the "whole truth." Beethoven is better than the Beatles, and Shakespeare greater than Noel Coward, because they incorporate the popular song and the popular play, and then transcend them; their larger truth does not deny the lesser truth but simply supersedes it. This does not mean that anyone can equal Beethoven or Shakespeare by simply adding up all the tunes or all the dramatic incidents one can think of. Genius remains the first premise; but once this premise is granted, the larger artistic truth is superior to the smaller. That is why, in "Tragedy and the Whole Truth" (1931), Huxley observes that "there is no contemporary writer of significance who does not prefer to state the Whole Truth. However different from one

117

another in style, in ethical, philosophical and artistic intention, in the scales of values accepted, contemporary writers have this in common, that they are interested in the Whole Truth. Proust, D. H. Lawrence, André Gide, Kafka, Hemingway—here are five obviously significant and important contemporary writers. Five authors as remarkably unlike one another as they could well be. They are at one only in this: that none of them has written a pure tragedy, that all are concerned with the Whole Truth." (*Music at Night*, 17).

Brave New World is too small in compass to state satisfactorily the whole truth, though it must be said in extenuation that it could not do so in any case because the future world it depicts has obliterated the concept of the whole truth. Truth, like man, in Huxley's new world is necessarily partial and incomplete. Nevertheless, in the fate of the Savage, in Lenina's tragic-comic love, in Helmholtz's struggle to move beyond poetic doggerel, in Bernard's social and amorous frustrations, Huxley hints at the larger truths he cannot fully express. And, of course, in its complexity of allusion, literary but also scientific and political, *Brave New World* turns out to be a remarkably wholly truthful work. Hence, whatever its inadequacies, this novel at least faces in the direction of the whole truth.

It is in this dedication to the whole truth, unrealizable though it may be, that *Brave New World* is unusual among utopian and anti-utopian fictions. It is this that has made it, in the words of George Kateb, the most influential anti-utopian novel of the twentieth century.[2] For, more than any other novel of its type, *Brave New World* is continuing to approximate the social and political whole truth as the present turns into the future, almost, one might say, to the point that a day can be foreseen when this novel will express the whole truth of a lamentably truth-impoverished time.

The only modern anti-utopian novel in English that rivals *Brave New World* in influence as well as in whole-truthfulness is George Orwell's *Nineteen Eighty-Four*. Ever since its publication in 1949, this novel has invited comparison, invidious and otherwise, with its great predecessor. Orwell himself was conscious of his debt when he sent Huxley a copy of his novel shortly after publication. Huxley replied with a letter full of praise, mingled, however, with a certain skepticism and with language that clearly evokes the foreword he had written for *Brave New World* three years earlier. *Nineteen Eighty-Four*, according to Huxley, is really about the "ultimate revolution," which was first proposed by the Marquis de Sade, who wished to consummate—to the most logically absurd degree—the revolution(s) begun by Babeuf and Robespierre. This is exactly what Huxley had said in his foreword in connection with the "really revolutionary revolution," but there de Sade is dismissed as a lunatic whose final aim was universal chaos and destruction. Not so, however, in the letter to Orwell. Here "the philosophy of the ruling minority in *Nineteen Eighty-Four* is a sadism which has been carried to its logical conclusion by going beyond sex and denying it" (L,604). This logical conclusion, however, is not based on a logic that Huxley is altogether prepared to accept. For Huxley, a sane sadism, as it were, was the starting point. On a permanent basis, so Huxley believes, the policy of the boot-on-the-face is not likely to succeed. In Napoleon's words, one can do everything with bayonets except sit on them. Hence Huxley considers that "the ruling oligarchy will find less arduous and wasteful ways of governing and of satisfying its lust for power, and that these ways will resemble those which I described in *Brave New World.*" The political system envisioned by *Nineteen Eighty-Four* is simply not efficient, and, all other things being equal, efficiency leads to stability as inefficiency leads away from it.

The letter to Orwell was not the last word Huxley had to say on the subject of *Nineteen Eighty-Four*. In *Themes and Variations* (1950), which he must have been finishing at the same time as he composed the letter to Orwell, Huxley seems rather less certain of himself.[3] "Sixteen years ago [actually seventeen or eighteen], when I wrote *Brave New World,*" Huxley tells us, "I fancied that the third revolution [that is, the really revolutionary or ultimate revolution] was still five or six centuries away. Today that estimate seems to be excessive. Mr. Orwell's forecast in *Nineteen Eighty-Four* was made from a vantage point considerably farther down the descending spiral of modern history than mine, and is more nearly correct. It may be indeed that he is completely right and that, only thirty-five years from now, the third revolution, whose crude beginnings are already visible, will be an accomplished fact—the most important and most terrible fact in human history" (127). The contradiction between this statement and what Huxley had written in his letter to Orwell seems blatant, but only, I think, superficially so. For here Huxley is not really concerned with the substance and character of the "third revolution," but only with its chronology; not with the what and wherefore, but only with the when. Orwell was right that it would come sooner rather than, as Huxley had once thought, later.[4]

Huxley's fullest evaluation of *Nineteen-Eighty-Four*, however, occurs in *Brave New World Revisited* (1959), which is so shot through with references to Orwell's novel that it might almost be called a justification of *Brave New World* in terms of *Nineteen Eighty-Four*. In his comments on Orwell's novel here, Huxley takes roughly the same line he had adopted in the letter to Orwell ten years earlier, while making the same reservations as in *Themes and Variations*. Unlike *Nineteen Eighty-Four*, Huxley maintains, *Brave New World* was written without the "benefit" of Hitlerism and (fully developed) Stalinism, and for that reason "the future dictatorship of my imaginary world was a good deal less brutal than the future dictatorship so brilliantly portrayed by Orwell" (12). From the perspective of 1948, the world of *Nineteen Eighty-Four* seemed very probable; but from the perspective of 1959, much less so. Soviet Russia after Stalin is no longer quite the brutal and terroristic state it had once been, and so, assuming that no atomic war intervened to destroy all calculations—and mankind—"it now looks as though the odds were more in favour of something like *Brave New World* than of something like *Nineteen Eighty-Four*" (13).

Again Huxley makes the point that terror is a less efficient administrative tool than pleasure; the stick less a guarantee of stability than the carrot. Enforced sexual abstinence, as in the case of Party Members in *Nineteen Eighty-Four*, may make sense in a world continually at war, but it is nonsense in a world at peace, in a world state such as that depicted in *Brave New World*. Besides, the lust for power can be equally well satisfied by inflicting a humiliating pleasure rather than a humiliating pain; and the power of pleasure has the advantage of being more stabilizing. Furthermore, the highest caste in a future dictatorship, whether along Orwell's lines or Huxley's own, can never be "tame"—that is, it can never be fully conditioned and brainwashed in the way the lower castes can, because the administrative caste must always retain the capacity to react to new and unexpected situations (96). If, however, the upper caste remains "wild," then there will always be the danger—and the hope—that it will act heretically and rebelliously. The hope, in other words, is not, as Orwell has it, in the "proles"; the hope is in the O'Briens. As long as there are O'Briens, Orwell's state must inevitably be unstable.

Whether Orwell ever replied to Huxley's letter is uncertain. In any event, no letter form Orwell has survived, perhaps because none was written or, perhaps, because it perished in the disastrous fire that destroyed all of Huxley's papers and books in 1961. It is a pity that no letter can be referred to, but it is not a desperate loss because *Nineteen Eighty-Four* is really in a number of fundamental respects a reply to *Brave New World*. It provides different answers to the same questions that had provoked Huxley to write his novel in the first place; it conducts a kind of dialogue between the lines with Huxley's novel.

At the same time it also conducts another dialogue with an earlier anti-utopian novel, Evgenii Zamiatin's *We*, which had appeared in English translation in 1924.[5] Orwell first came across Zamiatin's book in 1944 in Gleb Struve's *Twenty-Five Years of Soviet Russian Literature*, then tracked it down and read it. He was interested in "that kind of book" because, as he wrote Struve in February 1944, he had been "making notes for one myself that may get written sooner or later."[6] Two years later he reviewed *We* for *The Tribune* and immediately made the connection with *Brave New World:* "The first thing anyone would notice about *We* is the fact—never before pointed out, I believe—that Aldous Huxley's *Brave New World* must be partly derived from it . . . the atmosphere of the two books is similar, and it is roughly speaking the same kind of society that is being described. . . ."[7] Three years later, at about the same time he was sending a copy of *Nineteen Eighty-Four* to Huxley, he made the identical connection in harsher terms while writing to F. J. Warburg: "I think Aldous Huxley's *Brave New World* must be plagiarized from it [*We*] to some extent."[8]

As a matter of fact Huxley had not read *We* at the time he was writing *Brave New World*. Huxley himself later denied it, and Zamiatin, naturally curious about the subject, confirmed this when he got the following answer through a common acquaintance:

"Drieu la Rochelle told me the other day that in the course of a conversation with Huxley he asked him whether he had read *We;* he had not read it which proves these ideas are in the air we breathe."[9]

What is significant here, I think, is not so much whether Huxley had or had not read *We*—though that is naturally interesting in itself. What is significant is Orwell's reaction to his supposed discovery that Huxley had used *We* as an unacknowledged source. Though Orwell provides no real evidence either in his review or in the letter to Warburg for such use, he at once leaps to the conclusion that it must exist, that *Brave New World* must have been "plagiarized" from *We*. There is such an unseemly glee in this hasty response and in the crude terms in which it is put that one's suspicions are immediately aroused:[10] Orwell, it would appear, is only too glad to lay at Huxley's door what he very well knows rests squarely at his own. It is almost as if by attracting attention to the alleged connection between Huxley and Zamiatin, he hoped to diminish somehow the connection between himself and Zamiatin. If Huxley could plagiarize, why not Orwell too?

What is more, by pushing Zamiatin into the foreground Orwell also, whether intentionally or not, tended to obscure the connection between his own novel and Huxley's. That such a connection undoubtedly exists—and had existed well before Orwell had ever heard of Zamiatin—is apparent from the following reference to Huxley in Orwell's novel, *Keep the Aspidistra Flying* (1936). The anti-hero of this novel, a man who works in a greasy little bookshop not too dissimilar to Mr. Charrington's junk shop in *Nineteen Eighty-Four*, mocks the socialism of another character as being tantamount in practice to "some kind of Aldous Huxley *Brave New World;* only not so amusing. Four hours a day in a model factory, tightening up bolt number 6003. Rations served out in greaseproof paper at the communal kitchen. Community-hikes from Marx Hostel to Lenin Hostel and back. Free abortion-clinics on all the corners."[11]

A less amusing *Brave New World*—that is not exactly a fair description of *Nineteen Eighty-Four*. But it is not an entirely inaccurate description either. A brave new world made unamusing, that is, a brave new world stood on its head, did provide one of the original inspirations for *Nineteen Eighty-Four*, so much the passage from *Keep the Aspidistra Flying* makes unmistakably clear. That there were other, possibly even stronger influences goes without saying: besides *We*, certainly the history of Soviet development in the late 1930s, as reflected for instance in Koestler's *Darkness at Noon*; Orwell's own disillusionment in the Spanish Civil War; the rise of Nazi Germany. Still, *Brave New World*, chronologically at least, comes first.

There are numerous resemblances between *Nineteen Eighty-Four* and *Brave New World*, both in a general way and in specific instances. Like Huxley, Orwell begins his novel with the life of a "factory" worker, Winston Smith, and with a description of a typical day in the "factory," in this case the Ministry of Truth, which manufactures and recycles the past—for Orwell the most important and reprehensible activity of his future world, just as genetic engineering and conditioning are for Huxley. Near the beginning of his novel Orwell also cites the three slogans of Oceania—War Is Peace; Freedom Is Slavery; Ignorance Is Strength—just as Huxley had introduced his novel with the tripartite slogan of the new world state.[12] The slogans of the two futures are very different, but both more or less explicitly hark back to the famous motto of the French Revolution. Orwell's Two Minutes Hate, also introduced early in *Nineteen Eighty-Four*, is reminiscent of Huxley's conditioning, as well as of the Solidarity Service which, in Oceanic terms, might be described as One Hour Love—again an instance of Orwell's turning *Brave New World* on its head. Just as Bernard Marx manages only an incomplete and partially simulated solidarity with his fellow orgy-porgians, so too Winston Smith finds himself unable to join in wholeheartedly in the communal hatred and has to fake at least part of it.

As different as the means of the two future states are, their overall structure and some of their ends are remarkably similar: both divide humanity into two classes: the governing and the governed, with the latter in each case allowed or forced to pass their lives in drugged or drunken stupor; both have restricted research in science and technology to narrow areas that seem to ensure the power and stability of the state, in Orwell's case to instruments of war and police repression. Both have obliterated the past and have destroyed all books that might bear witness to it, though in Huxley's world state the past has officially ceased to be recognized at all, whereas in *Nineteen Eighty-Four* the past still survives, though not necessarily the past as it actually occurred. Both states rely heavily on conditioning to guarantee the orthodoxy of the administrative caste, with Oceania using chiefly continuous propaganda, youth organizations, "double-think" and related thought control. Such conditioning is clearly less efficient than that of Huxley's new world state, but there are indications that Oceania is moving consciously, in this respect at least, in the direction of a brave new world; so "New-speak" is being developed to the point where it will be impossible to think unorthodox thoughts because—as in the case of Helmholtz and even Lenina—there will be no words to think them in. So too in the Oceanic Junior Anti-Sex League, which already commits its members to bearing children by artificial insemination and to raising those children in public institutions, a program that in the further future envisioned by O'Brien will be made universal. This future is almost exactly that of the new world state stood on its head: a civilization founded not on pleasure, but on pain; not on "love," but on hatred. The Oceanic present, O'Brien tells Winston Smith, is still imperfect: "But in the future there will be no wives and no friends. Children will be taken from their mothers at birth, as one takes eggs from a hen. The sex instinct will be eradicated. Procreation will be an annual formality like the renewal of a ration card. We shall abolish the orgasm. Our neurologists are at work upon it now. There will be no loyalty, except loyalty towards the Party. There will be no love, except the love of Big Brother. There will be no laughter, except the laugh of triumph over a defeated enemy. There will be no art, no literature, no science. . . . . All competing pleasures will be destroyed. But always—do not forget this, Winston—always there will be the intoxication of power, constantly increasing and constantly growing subtler" (273). O'Brien's aim, in other words, is to produce, "neurologically" and by means of intense conditioning, a "new man," a man almost as new as the genetically engineered and scientifically conditioned new man of Huxley's novel.

The intoxication of power is the equivalent, in Huxley's future world, of the intoxications of sex and soma. These are very different intoxications, but they are different—or opposite—in the way two sides of the same coin are different and opposite. In both cases, man must be intoxicated. For Orwell, the most potent intoxicant is power; for Huxley—at least at the time he wrote *Brave New World*—it is sex. But for Orwell, as for Huxley, only a state that takes the ultimate intoxicant into prime consideration can achieve stability. The choice of power leads to a stability based on repression; the choice of sex, to a stability based on license. The final aim is the same; only the means are different.

Without presuming to decide which choice is the truer in any future or present context, I find it interesting to note that the two alternatives neatly reflect the two basic drives in the human psyche as analyzed by Freud. Huxley's future world is one in which the libido is liberated and allowed to run wild. Orwell's future world, on the other hand, has utterly repressed the libido in order to devote itself entirely to the death wish. Everything in Orwell's state leads to death: continuous warfare, public executions, systematic annihilation of the past, torture, vaporizings of heretics and orthodox alike. This atmosphere—worse, this stench—of death hangs so heavily over Orwell's world that one feels the most important of all the slogans is missing from the list of Oceanic mottos: Life Is Death.

The chief representative of Death is the Cain-like and mythical Big Brother. But as far as the plot of the novel itself is concerned, Death's name is O'Brien. O'Brien is in some ways curiously reminiscent of Mustapha Mond. Like Mond, he has immense power, but carries that power lightly and even "humbly," mingling as he does with his subjects on apparently equal terms. Like Mond, he is willing up to a point to engage in debate on the merits of his system and even to assign readings hostile to it (Emmanuel Goldstein's "The Book"), just as Mond cites Maine de Biran and Cardinal Newman. Like Mond, he seems to be, some of the time at least, a reasonable man, granted his premises about human nature and a society best designed to accommodate it. That he actively tortures Winston Smith makes him seem very different from Mond, but Mond too, one should remember, would be prepared to kill deviants if there were no islands to which they could be exiled.

The most striking resemblance between Mond and O'Brien, however, is the reaction each has to a particular rebel against the social order. In Mond's case, his interest in the Savage is explicitly justified as that of an experimenter with his "experiment"; he wants to see what happens when an intelligent, unconditioned, and sup-

posedly uncivilized human being is confronted with a social system
utterly foreign to his values. O'Brien's interest in Winston Smith is
more complex. He tells Winston, among other things, that he finds
his mind interesting because it so much resembles his own; Winston, in other words, functions as a kind of alter ego for O'Brien.
But even so there is a strong "experimental" aspect to their relationship. This is most obvious in the actual experiment of trying
and succeeding in making Winston betray Julia and even love Big
Brother, but it is evident in more subtle ways as well.

Toward the close of the novel it becomes clear that O'Brien has
been keeping Winston under surveillance for seven years, long
before the time Winston had committed his first overt act of rebellion in buying the cream-colored book. Though O'Brien never
admits it unambiguously, it seems clear that he must have been
deliberately influencing Winston's dream-life during this time.
Winston's dream of a voice that he later identifies with O'Brien's
telling him that "we shall meet in the place where there is no
Darkness" (i.e., in the cellar of the Ministry of Love) is a dream
that he dreamed precisely seven years earlier (250). The temporal
coincidence is obviously significant, as is O'Brien's lack of surprise
when Winston tells him of the dream. The point of all this, I think,
is that we are to conclude that Winston's deviant behavior has been
foreseen and even planned by O'Brien, that even his rebellion is
not his own—much as the rocket attacks on London are not caused
by the enemy but by the Party itself. If this is true, and all the
evidence suggests that it must be, then Winston's rebellion as well
as his "cure" are parts of an "experiment" carried out by O'Brien.
O'Brien, then, like Mond, becomes a kind of quasi-omnipotent
social scientist conducting his experiments on living human victims. Both are the executors of the third revolution.

Huxley's and Orwell's future states are alike in abominating
nothing more than the individual, and the plots of both novels are
fundamentally accounts of how individuals or potential individuals
are destroyed, exiled, or made to conform. The principal means for
achieving these ends is to substitute for reality a fiction that then
becomes absolute. Fiction-as-reality can be controlled and
manipulated in a way that reality—always fluid and unpredict-
able—cannot. Orwell's Ministry of Truth is the supreme instance
of the factory of fiction-as-reality and it is therefore fittingly

situated at the center of his state; but Huxley's new world also uses all its power to shield its citizens from the intimations of any reality other than that which they are conditioned to perceive. Bright lights and electric advertisements hide the night, and continuous noise drowns out any possible silence.

Winston Smith is in some respects strongly evocative of the principal characters of Huxley's novel. Like Bernard Marx, Winston Smith is an unattractive weakling, unsure of himself and unsure especially of how to deal with women. But the resemblance with Bernard is superficial. The deeper resemblance is to the Savage. Both Smith and the Savage are devoted to the past. Though Smith has no Shakespeare to fall back on, he cherishes mementos of the past like his diary and the crystal paperweight; he seeks also to recover the past in rhymes like those about the bells of the London churches. He also loves his mother—and even, like the Savage, feels a profound guilt at somehow having brought about her death. But more than any of these details, Winston resembles the Savage in being the last genuine human being. This is what Winston feels himself to be, and O'Brien even tells him in so many words that he is the last of the "old" human beings. Whether this is really true or not makes no difference. After all, there may be real human beings left with real families and real vivaporous children in exile on remote islands in Huxley's future world as well. What matters is that Winston, like the Savage, is convinced that he is the last of his kind. It is this conviction that makes their endings—preceded in both cases by betrayals of their inmost selves—so moving and tragic.

Nevertheless Winston lacks the heroic dimension of the Savage—lacks it, I think, because finally in *1984*, as perhaps in Orwell's own mind, there is no God. There are only echoes of God, only the distant ringing of church bells. For Orwell Satan in the person of O'Brien is not only supreme but unrivaled. Hence Winston's betrayal of Julia and of his own humanity reveals a pessimism on Orwell's part about the human condition that goes far beyond the skeptical Huxley's. Huxley's Savage, despite the betrayal of his inmost beliefs, holds fast to the essential core of those beliefs and this adherence gives his death meaning. In the Savage we can still see Christ. In Winston Smith there is only a Christ who has sold out to the devil.

There are a few other similarities between *Brave New World* and *Nineteen Eighty-Four* as well—the caste systems, the hierarchical society, the rejection of machines in favor of human labor—but enough has been said, I think, to show that Orwell was profoundly influenced by Huxley's novel when he composed his own.[13] This is not to diminish Orwell's achievement. Huxley himself was influenced by a whole variety of literary, political, and scientific works, and *Brave New World* is only the richer for it. So too with *Nineteen Eighty-Four* and Huxley's influence. Great works of art absorb their influences and are nourished by them; it is only lesser works of art that are impoverished by influence.

Finally, it must be said that the influence of *Brave New World*, like that of *Nineteen Eight-Four*, has not been merely and narrowly or even primarily literary. *Brave New World* is one of those works of literature that give the lie to W. H. Auden's assertion, in his great elegy "In Memory of W. B. Yeats," that "poetry makes nothing happen." Poetry, literature, art do or at least can make something happen, or, as in the case of *Brave New World* and *Nineteen Eighty-Four* help to prevent something from happening. These novels have shown us what may occur and have thereby given us an opportunity, however slight, to stop these particular versions of the future from being realized. If we do not find ourselves farther down the road to brave new world or 1984 than we now are, part of our gratitude should go to Huxley and Orwell. And if and when we actually do enter those new and terrible worlds, it will at least be with our eyes open.

Notes

A Note on the Notes

Unless indicated otherwise, references to publications by Aldous Huxley are to the Collected Works Edition, or, where not available, to the first Chatto & Windus edition. In all such cases page numbers are included in the text, preceded in ambiguous cases by a brief identifying title. *L*, followed by a page number, refers to the *Letters of Aldous Huxley*, ed. Grover Smith (London: Chatto & Windus, 1969).

Where it has seemed to add to the clarity of the argument, I have included the date of first publication for works by Huxley and others.

Chapter 1. The Future as Literature

1. But if *Brave New World* is indebted to *The Waste Land*, as Grover Smith has pointed out in *T. S. Eliot's Poetry and Plays: A Study in Sources and Meaning* (Chicago: University of Chicago Press, 1956), p. 76, then Eliot owes Madame Sosostris to Huxley's *Crome Yellow*.

2. For studies of Huxley's use of Shakespeare in *Brave New World*, see R. H. Wilson, "*Brave New World* as Shakespeare Criticism," *The Shakespeare Association Bulletin* 21 (July 1946): 99–107; Jerome Meckier, "Shakespeare and Aldous Huxley," *Shakespeare Quarterly* 22 (Spring 1971): 129–35; and J. A. A. Powell, "The Vanishing Values—Huxley's Permutations of *The Tempest*," Ph.D. diss., University of Utah, 1973. Some of Huxley's allusions are not literary at all but purely personal and even whimsical, as for instance the description of Eton College, which Huxley had attended himself and where he had taught at the end of the first World War. Miss Keate, the headmistress, derives her name from John Keate (1773–1852), an Eton headmaster who was infamous for the scale and severity of his beatings. So too the "Aphroditeum" alludes to the Athenaeum, an elite London club to which Huxley belonged and where he often stayed while visiting London.

3. Donald Watt, "The Manuscript Revisions of *Brave New World*," *Journal of English and Germanic Philology* 77(July 1978): 380.

4. *Virginia Quarterly Review* 7 (January 1931): 49, 53. Some of the same ideas are broached in D. H. Lawrence's essay, "Men Must Work and Women as Well," dating from November 1929. This suggests that Huxley and Lawrence were talking along these lines as early as mid-1929 or even earlier. For a more detailed discussion of Lawrence's essay, see chapter 3.

5. As, for example, in *Crome Yellow*.

6. Watt, "Manuscript," pp. 374, 377.

7. The mention of Stoke Poges is probably intended to evoke in the reader's mind the "Elegy Written in a Country Churchyard," whose author lies buried there. For another and fuller parodic allusion to the same poem, see Malinda Snow, "The Gray Parody in *Brave New World*," *Papers on Language and Literature* 13 (Winter 1977): 85.

8. Notably Jerome Meckier in "A Neglected Huxley 'Preface': His Earliest Synopsis of *Brave New World*," *Twentieth Century Literature*, 25 (Spring 1979), 7–8, but also Watt, "Manuscript," 375.

9. According to Theodor W. Adorno's "Aldous Huxley und die Utopie" (1942; 1951), Bernard Marx is "a skeptically sympathetic caricature of a Jew." (my translation). This idea, aside from being absurd in itself in the context of *in vitro* generation, fails to take into account that Huxley had earlier portrayed non-Jewish characters with remarkably similar traits, such as Illidge in *Point Counter Point*. See the reprint of this essay in Adorno's *Prismen* (Berlin: Suhrkamp, [1955]), p. 127.

10. Aside from satirizing Freud here, Huxley may also be mocking Shaw. In the fourth part of Shaw's interminable utopian fantasy, *Back to Methuselah*, there is the following (quite serious) interchange: "*Elderly Gentleman*. People will think I am your father. *The Man* [shocked]. Sh-sh! People here never allude to such relationships. It is not quite delicate, is it?" The idea of prudish supermen must have tickled Huxley's satiric nerve, though one critic at least, considers Shaw's play as providing a "mystical vision . . . wholly outside the range" of Huxley's novel. See Georg Roppen, *Evolution and Poetic Belief* (Oslo: Oslo University Press, 1956), p. 454. In the fifth and final part of the play, "As Far as Thought Can Reach," Shaw's supermen and superwomen are born out of eggs, spend their youth in pastoral dalliance, and then turn into "Ancients" whose only interest consists in contemplating their navels and exterminating newly-hatched members of the community who are biologically unfit. To this sad height has creative evolution led us. And one day, so Shaw foretells, our ancient descendants will leap from that height to become like unto gods, at least to the extent of being deathless and immaterial: "*The Newly Born*. What is your destiny? *The He-Ancient*. To be immortal. *The She-Ancient*. The day will come when there will be no people, only thought." This emphasis on pure consciousness and self-consciousness indicates Shaw's debt to Plato via Hegel. Huxley, of course, ridicules the idea of creative evolution—and, implicitly, Shaw as one of its leading exponents—by showing that man is not its vehicle but its master. He is able to stop evolution by technological means whenever he chooses. Man is not merely the measure of all things, he is the measurer; and in *Brave New World* he takes his own sadly Procrustean measure. See George Bernard Shaw, *Complete Plays* (London: Constable, 1931), p. 914 and p. 958.

11. Huxley admired Voltaire greatly and even possessed a first edition of *Candide*. See his essay, "On Re-reading *Candide*" (1923) in *On the Margin* (London: Chatto & Windus, 1956), p. 12. The connection between *Candide* and Huxley's Savage was first pointed out by Charlotte Haldane in her review of *Brave New World*, "Dr. Huxley and Mr. Arnold," *Nature* 129 (23 April 1932): 598.

12. There is a distinct possibility that Huxley may have had Gustave Flaubert's *La Tentation de Saint Antoine* in mind while writing the conclusion of *Brave New World*. Flaubert describes several scenes of flagellation, but one with especial relish. After glimpsing seductive visions among the rocks, St. Anthony turns to the whip for punishment. He whips himself until he finds it pleasurable, then harder to punish himself for that pleasure. Lascivious memories of a girl he had known in his youth float through his mind, and as a consequence the whip comes down harder still, until he finally climaxes in a kind of flagellatory orgasm. See Gustave Flaubert, *La Tentation de Saint Antoine* (Paris: Louis Conard,

1924), pp. 28–29. In this connection, it is perhaps also worth noting that the sign of the T— Our Ford's religious symbol—is technically known as St. Anthony's Cross.

13. Aldous Huxley, "Brave New World," *Life* 25 (20 September 1948): 63–64, 66–68, 70.

14. This emphasis on permanent youthfulness (or permanent adolescence) derives in part from the fact that Huxley is parodying Wells's preoccupation with such matters in *Men Like Gods* (1923). See my more detailed discussion in chapter 3. There is, of course, a very old tradition that envisions eternal youth under utopian conditions: the story of Adam and Eve is probably the oldest of such visions but there is also the paradise of Hesiod's *Works and Days*. In British Utopian fiction before Wells, Bulwer Lytton had depicted in *The Coming Race* (1871) a society of subterranean supermen who live with their vitality virtually unimpaired until the age of 150. This is made possible by a quasi-magical substance known as "vril," which also has some of the characteristics of Huxley's soma. Bulwer-Lytton also anticipates Huxley's novel in such matters as hypnopaedia and modified sexual promiscuity. The details of the hypnopaedic technique itself, however, Huxley seems to have drawn principally from F. W. H. Myers, *Human Personality and Its Survival of Bodily Death* (New York: Longman, 1904), 1:172–74.

In the early years of the century a good deal of attention was aroused by rejuvenation techniques, such as those of Steinach and Voronoff. Huxley refers to the Steinach operation (which W. B. Yeats was later to undergo) in *On the Margin*, p. 106, where he speculates that it may lead to a future in which age and decay have no place. For a more detailed treatment of this subject, see Philip Gibbs, *The Day After To-morrow* (London:Hutchinson [1927]), pp. 69–73.

15. Passages from *The Brothers Karamazov* are quoted from the New American Library Edition, trans. Constance Garnett (New York, 1957). Rebecca West noted the connection between Dostoevski's novel and Huxley's when she reviewed the latter for the *Daily Telegraph* on February 5, 1932. In the final chapter of *Brave New World Revisited* (1958), Huxley makes a similar allusion (pp. 162–63). Dostoevski may also have exercised an influence on *Brave New World* through his satire of the utopian ideas of Shigalev and Pyotr Verkhovensky in *The Possessed*, a novel that shaped some of the characters and events of *Point Counter Point*.

16. In *Those Barren Leaves* Huxley provides a less complete and imaginative reworking of the parable of the Grand Inquisitor. It takes the form of a brief catechism that sums up the cynicism of the anti-hero, Francis Chelifer, and concludes as follows (p. 107): "*Q*. On what condition can I live a life of contentment? *A*. On the condition that you do not think. *Q*. What is the function of newspapers, cinemas, radios, motorbikes, jazz bands, etc.? *A*. The function of these things is the prevention of thought and the killing of time. They are the most powerful instruments of human happiness. *Q*. What did the Buddha consider the most deadly of the deadly sins? *A*. Unawareness, stupidity."

17. Aldous Huxley, "The Outlook for American Culture: Some Reflections in a Machine Age," *Harper's Magazine* 155 (August 1927): 265–70.

Chapter 2. The Future of Science and Our Freud

1. Russell especially had a wonderful opportunity to put in a claim for priority when he reviewed *Brave New World* for the *New Leader* on 11 March 1932, but he did nothing of the sort. Instead he praised the novel highly and concluded that a brave new world was inevitable if the contemporary world continued to progress along its present course. See the reprint of this review in Donald Watt, ed., *Aldous Huxley: The Critical Heritage* (London: Routledge & Kegan Paul, 1975), p. 212.

2. G. R. Taylor, *The Biological Time-Bomb* (London: Panther Books, 1972), p. 43.

3. J. B. S. Haldane, "Biological Possibilities for the Human Species in the Next Ten Thousand Years," in *Man and His Future*, ed. Gordon Wolstenholme (London: J. & A. Churchill, 1963), p. 340.

4. Gerald Leach, *The Biocrats* (London: Jonathan Cape, 1970), p. 151. According to Lewis Mumford's *The Pentagon of Power*, vol. 2 of *The Myth of the Machine* (New York: Harcourt, Brace, Jovanovich, 1970), pp. 224ff., the predictions of *Brave New World* have already been realized.

5. Joseph Needham, "Biology and Mr. Huxley," *Scrutiny* 1 (May 1932): 76; H. V. Routh, *English Literature and Ideas in the Twentieth Century* (London: Methuen, 1946), p. 182; Philip Thody, *Aldous Huxley* (London: Studio Vista, 1973), pp. 50–51.

6. Ronald Clark, *JBS* (London: Hodder & Stoughton, 1968), p. 70.

7. Julian Huxley, ed., *Aldous Huxley, 1894–1963* (London: Chatto & Windus, 1965), p. 22.

8. In *An Occupation for Gentlemen* (London: Hutchinson, 1959), pp. 109–13, the publisher Fredric Warburg recounts how C. K. Ogden urged Routledge to publish *Daedalus*, which "received glowing reviews and made an impact on the public which was electrifying," selling some twenty thousand copies. Russell was then invited to reply in *Icarus*, which also sold well. This success decided Routledge to start the "Today and Tomorrow" Series, in which "most of the titles were classical names, and the device worked well. The series continued in full spate for six years and more, an unprecedented time for what were really short essays."

9. Clark, *JBS,* p. 70.

10. J. B. S. Haldane, *Daedalus* (New York: Dutton, 1942), pp. 22, 34–37, 64, and 73. The first mention of ectogenesis as a possible method of human reproduction occurs in Denis Diderot's *Rêve de'Alembert*, which Huxley may have known. See the edition by Paul Vernière (Paris: Marcel Didier, 1951), pp. lvii–lviii and 52–54. Historically, the Italian scientist, L. Spallanzini, was the first to practice artificial insemination successfully in animals. This was carried out on a bitch in 1780, whereupon his friend Charles Bonnet wrote to him: "I do not even know if what you have just discovered will not some day have applications for the human species which we do not dream of and whose consequences will not be slight" (my translation). In 1799 the English surgeon W. Hunter succeeded in artificially inseminating a woman. See Jean Rostand, *Science et Génération* (Paris: Fasquelle, 1948), pp. 16–17. There is a possibility that Huxley may have been indirectly influenced by H. J. Muller, the Nobel Prize-winning geneticist who became a lifelong friend of Julian Huxley's after assisting him at Rice in 1912. Muller's *Out of the Night* was not published until 1936, but in his preface Muller claims the book was essentially complete by 1910. Huxley praises Muller and his concern with eugenics in *The Human Situation* (New York: Harper & Row, 1977), p. 105. The so-called Bokanovsky process—what we nowadays call cloning—is a genuine anticipation on Huxley's part of later developments in genetics, though some work had already been done in this area by the 1920s. E. M. Conklin's *Heredity and Environment* (Princeton, N.J.: Princeton University Press, 1922), p. 227, describes an experiment in which, provided "the cleavage cells are only partially separated they may produce animals which are partially separated. . . . Or these double monsters may be produced by division or budding of the embryo at a later stage of development." "Budding" is also the world Huxley uses in connection with the Bokanovsky process. In his review of *Brave New World* in *Scrutiny*, Joseph Needham explicitly accepts the possibility of this kind of biological innovation. Also H. S. Jennings, *Prometheus, Or Biology and the Advancement of Man* (London: Kegan Paul, [1926], p. 88, maintains that "what the eugenic plan requires is that the adult, after he has shown his value, should be multiplied without change of genetic combination. If

this could be done, man would have his fate in his hands. He could multiply the desirable population until the entire population consisted of that type."

Brave New World was not the first fictional application of Haldane's ectogenesis. J. D. Bernal's *The World, The Flesh and the Devil* (1929)—a positive or "plus" utopia—depicts a world in which reproduction is *in vitro*, adolescence occurs between the ages of sixty and one hundred and twenty, which is then followed by transplanation to a plastic body and a maturity devoted to contemplation. Bernal's future world seems a fusion of Haldane and Shaw.

11. Charlotte Haldane, "Dr. Huxley and Mr. Arnold", *Nature* 129 (23 April 1932): 598. Rather odd, after this fulsome praise is J. B. S. Haldane's claim in his draft autobiography that his wife "avenged Rosie [the unfaithful wife of Shearwater-Haldane in *Antic Hay*] by reviewing *Brave New World* in *Nature*." See Clark, *JBS*, p. 57. It is worth adding, however, that the concept of neotonous development that Huxley employs in *After Many a Summer* is anticipated by Haldane in *Science and Human Life* (New York: Harper, 1933), p. 33; and that the social changes pursuant to human rut, later elaborated by Huxley in *Ape and Essence*, are already broached in Haldane's *Possible Worlds* (New York: Harper, 1928), p. 286.

12. Bertrand Russell, *Icarus* (London: Kegan Paul, 1924), p. 54.

13. Bertrand Russell, *The Scientific Outlook* (Glencoe, Ill.: The Free Press, 1931), pp. 214, 184, 195, 242, 248–49, 255.

14. Ibid., p. 259.

15. It is a pity that Huxley's letters to Russell and Haldane are not included in the recent edition of his correspondence. Much light may be shed on the scientific background of his fiction when these finally become available.

16. Gustave LeBon, *The Crowd* (London: Fisher Unwin, 1896), pp. 118–20.

17. Haldane, *Daedalus*, p. 14.

18. Useful for further background are J. S. Haldane, *Mechanism, Life and Personality* (London: John Murray, 1913); J. J. von Uexkuell, *Theoretical Biology* (London: Kegan Paul, 1926); Joseph Needham, *Man a Machine* (London: Kegan Paul, 1927); and J. H. Woodger, *Biological Principles* (New York: Harcourt, Brace & Co., 1929). Under the guise of the mind-body problem, the controversy has continued down to the present day; see John Beloff's "The Mind-Body Problem As It Now Stands," *Virginia Quarterly Review* 49 (Spring 1973): 251–64.

19. Lancelot Hogben, *The Nature of Living Matter* (New York: Knopf, 1931), p. 79.

20. Ibid., p. 90.

21. John B. Watson, *Behaviorism*, 2d ed. (London: Kegan Paul, 1931), p. 104. According to Henshaw Ward, *Builders of Decision* (Indianapolis: Bobbs-Merrill, 1931), p. 262, Watson's *Behaviorism* was enormously successful in the United States: "the critics surrendered to him, speaking thus in New York reviews: 'Perhaps *Behaviorism* is the most important book ever written.' 'It marks an epoch in the intellectual history of man.'"

22. John B. Watson and William McDougall, *The Battle of Behaviorism* (London: Kegan Paul, 1928), pp. 26–27.

23. George Orwell, *The Road to Wigan Pier* (London: Heinemann, 1965), p. 192. Huxley's friend J. W. N. Sullivan's *Gallio or the Tyranny of Science* (London: Kegan Paul, [1927]), p. 58, contends that the only possible response to Behaviorism "is a satire, as when Voltaire answered the theory that in this world everything is for the best in the best of all possible worlds by writing *Candide*."

24. See also J. W. N. Sullivan's *The Limitations of Science* (London: Chatto & Windus, 1933), p. 176, for confirmation of this.

25. Thody, *Huxley*, p. 55.

26. Sigmund Freud, *Works*, vol. 21, trans. James Strachey (London: Hogarth, 1961), pp. 7, 47–48, 56. In "Aldous Huxley und die Utopie" (1942; 1951), the German critic and sociologist Theodor W. Adorno censures Huxley for using Freud as one of the butts of his satire. Huxley, according to Adorno, reduces Freud to "a mere efficiency expert of the inner life. He is mocked in all too easy a way for having been the first to discover 'the appalling dangers of family life.' But, in fact, that is just what he did and the verdict of history is on his side . . . ." (my translation). Oddly enough, Adorno also objects to Huxley's thesis that culture and happiness are not reconcilable, without seeming to realize that here Huxley and Freud are in perfect agreement. See Adorno's *Prismen* (Berlin: Suhrkamp, [1955]), p. 123.

27. Ibid., pp. 76–78.

28. Ibid., p. 96.

29. Ibid., p. 49.

30. Aldous Huxley, "Obstacle Race," *The Adelphi* (April 1931), p. 40.

31. For a different but complementary view of Huxley's understanding of Freud, see Jerome Meckier's "Our Ford, Our Freud and the Behaviorist Conspiracy in Huxley's *Brave New World*," *Thàlia* 1 (1977–78): 35–59.

32. S. D. Schmalhausen, *Why We Misbehave* (Garden City, N.Y.: Garden City Publishing Co., 1928), pp. 30, 34, 41.

33. Dora Russell, *The Right to Be Happy* (London: Routledge & Sons, 1927), pp. 128–32, 153–55, 168, 177, 248, 280. This attack on the family is not new. In *The Origin of the Family*, Friedrich Engels had already denounced the family as a new, unnecessary, and reactionary institution. See also A. M. Ludovici, *Lysistrata or Woman's Future and Future Woman* (London: Kegan Paul, [1926]), pp. 86–96.

34. Bertrand Russell, *Marriage and Morals* (London: Allen & Unwin, 1929), pp. 9, 264–65, 270.

35. Bertrand Russell, *The Conquest of Happiness* (New York: The Book League of America, 1930), p. 19.

36. Douglas Goldring, *Odd Man Out* (London: Chapman & Hall, 1935), p. 227.

37. V. F. Calverton and S. D. Schmalhausen, eds., *Sex in Civilization* (New York: Macmillan, 1929), p. 435.

38. In the Freudian schemata the notion of restraint is identified with the so-called reality principle which, "without giving up the intention of ultimately attaining pleasure yet demands and enforces the postponement of satisfaction, the renunciation of manifold possibilities of it, and the temporary endurance of 'pain' on the long and circuitous road to pleasure." From "Beyond the Pleasure Principle" (1920), in Sigmund Freud, *A General Selection from the Works*, ed. John Rickman (Garden City, N.Y.: Doubleday, 1957), pp. 142–43.

Chapter 3. From Savages to Men Like Gods

1. George Wickes and Ray Frazer, "Aldous Huxley," *Writers at Work, The "Paris Review" Interviews*, 2d ser. (London: Secker & Warburg, 1963), p. 165. That Huxley knew and in some sense admired Wells's scientific fantasies is confirmed by his essay, "If My Library Burned Tonight," *Home and Garden* 92 (November 1947): 243. It is perhaps also worth noting that *Men Like Gods* was reviewed in *Nature* by Julian Huxley, who was later to collaborate with Wells on *The Science of Life* (1931).

2. Derek Patmore, *Private History* (London: Jonathan Cape, 1960), p. 154. Patmore goes on to describe how Wells, "ever an ardent socialist . . . was certain that social progress would cure the evils that men were so easily prone to, and when we discussed the works of such

writers as Aldous Huxley he said to me savagely: '*Brave New World* was a great disappointment to me. A writer of the standing of Aldous Huxley has no right to betray the future as he did in that book. When thinking about the future, people seem to overlook the logical progress in education, in architecture, in science.'" H. G. Wells, *The New World Order* (New York: Knopf, 1940), p. 126; and Klaus Mann, *Der Wendepunkt, Ein Lebensbericht* (Frankfurt am Main: Fischer, 1952), p. 439. Huxley and Wells did, however, continue to correspond occasionally, and in late 1933 Huxley even joined Wells as one of the Vice-Presidents of the Federation of Progressive Societies and Individuals.

3. H. G. Wells, *Seven Famous Novels* (Garden City, N.Y.: Garden City Publishing Company, 1934), p. ix.

4. Quoted in W. Warren Wagar, *H. G. Wells and the World State* (New Haven, Conn.: Yale University Press, 1961), p. 48.

5. H. G. Wells, *Tales of Space and Time* (Leipzig: Tauchnitz, 1900), pp. 240–41.

6. H. G. Wells, *Men Like Gods* (New York: Macmillan, 1923), p. 266.

7. Ibid., p. 291.

8. H. G. Wells, *When the Sleeper Wakes* (New York: Harper's, 1899), pp. 69, 167, 216.

9. Mark Hillegas, *The Future as Nightmare, H. G. Wells and the Anti-Utopians* (New York: Oxford, 1967), pp. 111ff. Huxley's fictional history of the new world state may derive from—and parody—Wells's brutal utopia, *The World Set Free* (1914), in which, just as in Huxley's novel, liberation only takes place after the world is utterly devastated. In Wells's case this occurs by means of atomic bombs, which keep on exploding and releasing radioactive vapor for decades, and so render the sometime principal cities of the world uninhabitable.

10. H. G. Wells, *The First Men in the Moon* (London: George Newnes, 1901), p. 304.

11. Gerald Heard, "The Poignant Prophet," *The Kenyon Review* 27 (Winter 1965): 57.

12. Hillegas, *Future*, p. 120.

13. Reprinted in *H. G. Wells, The Critical Heritage*, ed. Patrick Parrinder (London: Routledge & Kegan Paul, 1972), p. 288.

14. Philip Gibbs, *The Day After Tomorrow* (London: Hutchinson, [1927]), p. 235.

15. D. H. Lawrence, *Selected Literary Criticism*, ed. Anthony Beal (London: Heinemann, 1955), p. 136.

16. D. H. Lawrence, *Poems* (Geneva: Heron, 1964), 1:501.

17. Julian Huxley, *Memories* (New York: Harper & Row, 1970), p. 160.

18. This essay has been reprinted in D. H. Lawrence, *Phoenix II*, ed. Warren Roberts and H. T. Moore (New York: Penguin, 1978), pp. 583–90.

19. Wickes, "Huxley," p. 165.

20. Aldous Huxley, preface to Knud Merrild, *A Poet and Two Painters* (London: George Routledge, 1938), p. xvi.

21. D. H. Lawrence, *Mornings in Mexico* (London: Martin Secker, 1927), p. 101. Huxley read this work in October 1927 and liked it.

22. D. H. Lawrence, *Phoenix*, ed. E. D. McDonald (London: Heinemann, 1936), pp. 144 and 142.

23. Aldous Huxley, "The Cold-Blooded Romantics," *Vanity Fair* 30 (March 1928): 104.

24. The name "Popé," however, alludes to Popé of San Juan, a leader in the great 1680 Pueblo Indian rebellion against the Spaniards. By "Smithsonian Reports" Huxley means the *Annual Report of the Bureau of Ethnology*, which since 1880 has frequently published detailed studies of Pueblo Indian culture, notably by Tilly E. Stevenson, J. P. Harrington, and Leslie A. White. For general information Huxley may also have relied on Pliny Earle Goddard's *Indians of the Southwest* (New York: American Museum of Natural History, 1913), which along which geographical and historical information contains a good description

of the Snake Dance. The nonexistent pueblo of "Malpais" in *Brave New World* does not resemble physically the Zuñi pueblo at Thunder Mountain, but rather the linguistically unrelated pueblo of Acoma, over which Bernard and Lenina fly on their way to Malpais. I have been unable to determine if all the Zuñi words that the Savage occasionally bursts out with are actually Zuñi. There are, however, some resemblances between the Savage's language and the samples of Zuñi given in Ruth L. Bunzel's *Zuñi Texts*, Publications of the American Ethnological Society, vol. 15 (New York: Stechert, 1933).

At least one of the words used by the Savage—*hani*—occurs in Frank Hamilton Cushing's *My Adventures in Zuni* (Santa Fé, N.M.: The Peripatetic Press, 1941), p. 134, originally published in 1922–23. The word is there glossed as a sister's younger brother. According to Stanley Newman's *Zuni Dictionary* (Bloomington: Indiana Research Center in Anthropology, Folklore and Linguistics, 1958), *hanni* means a sister's younger sibling. The Savage appears to use the word as an insult, a usage not confirmed by either Cushing or Newman.

Huxley may also have consulted Cushing's "Outlines of Zuni Creation Myths," *Annual Report of the Bureau of Ethnology* 18 (1891–92): 325–447, for some of the Pueblo names and legends.

25. Elsie Clewes Parsons, *Pueblo Indian Religion* (Chicago: University of Chicago Press, 1939), 1:159.

26. H. K. Haeberlin, "The Idea of Fertilization in the Culture of the Pueblo Indians," *Memoirs of the American Anthropological Association* 3 (1916): 24 and 234. Goddard, *Indians*, p. 118, uses the spelling "Pookong," as Huxley does.

27. Elliot Fay, *Lorenzo in Search of the Sun* (London: Vision Press, 1955), p. 71.

28. There are other echoes of the Christ story as well. Helmholtz Watson's joining the Savage to fight the Deltas recalls Peter's defense of Christ, just as Bernard Marx's later attempt at disassociation recalls his betrayal. The identification with Christ among the Penitentes is immediate and explicit. One of the members is chosen to bear the cross, upon which he is later bound and raised. See Ruth Benedict, *Patterns of Culture* (London: Routledge & Sons, 1935), pp. 90–91.

Chapter 4. The Politics of Anti-Utopia

1. Granville Hicks, "Review of *Brave New World*," *The New Republic* 69 (February 10, 1932): 354.

2. Wells, as quoted in Mark Hillegas, *The Future as Nightmare* (New York: Oxford University Press, 1967), p. 121; J. D. Bernal, *The Social Function of Science* (Cambridge, Mass.: MIT Press, 1967), p. 381 (first published in 1939); Harold J. Laski, *Faith, Reason and Civilisation* (London: Gollancz, 1944), p. 112; and George Orwell, *Collected Essays, Journalism, and Letters*, ed. Sonia Orwell and Ian Angus (London: Secker & Warburg, 1968), 4:72–73.

3. Judith N. Shklar, *After Utopia* (Princeton, N.J.: Princeton University Press, 1957), p. 156; and Hillegas, *Future*, p. 120. So too C. Moody argues in "Zamiatin's *We* and English Antiutopian Fiction," *UNISA English Studies* 14 (1976): 28, that "to Huxley the most significant features of the present were not political. His villain is not Marx or Lenin, but Ford."

4. This worship of the machine is also characteristic of Italian fascism, which inherited it from Marinetti's Futurism. Part of the Futurist program was the destruction of the past— Marinetti advised his followers to blow up all museums—just as the new world state has destroyed the past.

5. Sir Walter Raleigh, Huxley's tutor at Oxford, had once suggested that he write a

dissertation on Greville, but Huxley's taste for the academic life was limited. His knowledge, however, of sixteenth- and seventeenth-century English dramatic literature was extensive, almost to the point of pedantry. Lenina Crowne's surname, for example, appears to refer to the Anglo-American restoration playwright John Crowne, best known for his play "Sir Courtly Nice, Or It Cannot Be" (1685), though Huxley may also have intended his readers to think of Crowne's *Calisto, or, The Chaste Nimph* (1675).

6. L. G. Crocker, *Rousseau's Social Contract: An Interpretive Essay* (Cleveland: Western Reserve, 1968), pp. 132 and 158n. According to J. L. Talmon, *The Origins of Totalitarian Democracy* (London: Secker & Warburg, 1952), p. 91, "Rousseau had said that man should be as independent as possible of any other person, and as dependent as possible on the state."

7. Judith N. Shklar, *Men and Citizens: A Study of Rousseau's Social Theory* (Cambridge: University Press, 1969), p. 170.

8. Quoted in ibid., p. 168.

9. Crocker, *Rousseau's*, pp. 136–37.

10. Shklar, *Men*, p. 202.

11. Jean-Jacques Rousseau, "Discours sur l'origine de l'inégalité parmi les hommes," in *Du Contrat social au principes du droit politique* (Paris: Garnier, 1962), p. 47.

12. For a brief treatment of Rousseau's ideal savage, see Frank E. and Fritzie P. Manuel, *Utopia in the Western World* (Cambridge: Harvard University Press, 1979), pp. 445–46. Very influential in shaping French Revolutionary ideas about noble savagery was also the Abbé Guillaume Raynal's *The Philosophical and Political History of the Indies* (1772). This work went through fifty-four editions before 1800. For more information see Carl L. Becker, *The Heavenly City of the Eighteenth-Century Philosophers* (New Haven, Conn.: Yale, 1959), p. 111.

13. "The Cold-Blooded Romantics," *Vanity Fair* 30 (March 1928): 104. Lawrence is not mentioned by name in this essay, but Huxley remedies this omission when he takes up the subject again in *Music at Night* (1931), p. 147. In the short story "Chawdron," in *Brief Candles* (1930), p. 21, Huxley's narrator is skeptical about the existence of Rousseau's and Shelley's "Natural Man." The really natural men are the primitives of Frazer and Malinowski, which means that "of course the savage isn't noble. Primitives are horrible."

14. In "Whither Are We Civilising?" *Vanity Fair* 30 (April 1928): 124, Huxley argues that "in modern societies the man, in Rousseau's words is sacrificed to the citizen," that is, "the instinctive and emotional man to the intellectually specialized citizen." See also *Music at Night*, p. 142, where the same argument is repeated in almost identical terms. In Huxley's mind the Savage may also be descended from Rousseau in other ways than noble savagery. In *Do What You Will* (1929), p. 134. Huxley ascribes the cult of romantic love—the kind of love the Savage feels for Lenina—to Rousseau. "It was Rousseau," so Huxley asserts, "who first started the cult of passion for passion's sake. . . . Rousseau, followed by all the romantic poets of France and England, transformed the grand passion from what it had been in the Middle Ages—a demoniac possession—into a divine ecstasy, and promoted it from the rank of a disease to that of the only true and natural form of love."

15. The connection between the moral laxity of Huxley's new world state and Mead's Samoa is particularly close, as may be appreciated from the following passage in *Coming of Age in Samoa* (New York: Blue Ribbon Books, 1932), p. 198: "The Samoan background which makes growing up so easy, so simple a matter, is the general casualness of the whole society. For Samoa is a place where no one plays for very high stakes, no one pays heavy prices, no one suffers for his convictions or fights to the death for special ends." For the original versions of the erotic games played by the Fordian children, see Bronislaw

Malinowski, *Sex and Repression in Savage Society* (New York: Harcourt, Brace & Co., 1927), p. 55.

16. Summarized by Lucio Colletti in *From Rousseau to Lenin: Studies in Ideology and Society* (London: NLB, 1972), pp. 145–46.

17. This fusion is aptly symbolized in the name of the leader of the Sixteen Sexophonists, Calvin Stopes.

18. F. E. Manuel and F. P. Manuel, eds., *French Utopias* (New York: The Free Press, 1966), pp. 275–77; and F. E. and F. P. Manuel, *Utopian Thought in the Western World* (Cambridge: Harvard University Press, 1979), p. 596.

19. Georges Dumas, *Psychologie de deux messies positivistes* (Paris: Félix Alcan, 1905), p. 2. My translation.

20. Manuel, *Utopian Thought*, p. 599. For the importance of psychology in the Saint-Simonian state, see also F. E. Manuel, *The New World of Saint-Simon* (Cambridge: Harvard University Press, 1956), p. 301.

21. Manuel, *French Utopias*, p. 8.

22. N. V. Riasanovsky, *The Teaching of Charles Fourier* (Berkeley: University of California Press, 1969), pp. 43–45, 55–60, 71–73.

23. Charles Fourier, *Design for Utopia*, ed. Charles Gide (New York: Schocken, 1971), pp. 167–68.

24. Manuel, *Utopian Thought*, pp. 659–61.

25. That the Soviet Union was on Huxley's mind while he was working on *Brave New World* is evident from his plans to tour that country with his brother, Julian, in the summer of 1931. These plans had to be canceled when Huxley ran into unexpected problems with his book (L, 348–49). M. D. Petre's "Bolshevist Ideals and the 'Brave New World,'" *The Hibbert Journal* 31 (October 1932–July 1933): 61–71, is of no intrinsic interest, but it does show that the first readers of *Brave New World* were aware that it was a critique of the Soviet Union.

26. Nicholas Berdyaev, *The End of Our Time* (London: Sheed & Ward, 1933), p. 191.

27. Ibid., p. 189.

28. René Fuelop-Miller, *The Mind and Face of Bolshevism* (New York: Harper & Row, 1965), p. 12.

29. Ibid., pp. 24, 31, 213.

30. The "dedicated *soma* tablets" and the "loving cup of strawberry ice-cream *soma*" are obviously references to the Christian communion, especially as practiced in American churches (hence the ice cream). The idea and name of soma Huxley derived from Indian myth, possibly via one of his favorite books, J. H. Leuba's *The Psychology of Religious Mysticism* (New York: Harcourt, Brace & Co., 1925), pp. 9–10. Here the origins and effects of soma are discussed in detail in a chapter entitled "Mystical Ecstasy As Produced by Physical Means." According to Leuba, "the drinking ceremony was accompanied by magical incantations and invocations," and "the desire for sexual vigour is one of the dominant notes of the soma hymns." Also, in "A Treatise on Drugs," *Chicago Herald and Examiner* (10 October 1931), 11, Huxley mentions reading a work on drugs by an unnamed "German pharmacologist."

31. Aldous Huxley, "Obstacle Race," *The Adelphi* (April 1931), p. 36.

32. Bertrand Russell, *Marriage and Morals* (London: Allen & Unwin, 1929), p. 5.

33. Panteleimon Romanof, *Without Cherry Blossom*, trans. L. Zarine (New York: Scribner's, 1932), p. 17.

34. Alexis de Tocqueville, *Democracy in America*, trans. Henry Reeve (New York: Colonial Press, 1899), 2:99, 239, and 276.

35. Ibid., pp. 332–33.

36. Colonel J. F. C. Fuller, *Atlantis, or America and the Future* (London: Kegan Paul, [1926]), p. 33.

37. Garet Garrett, *Ouroboros, Or the Mechanical Extension of Mankind* (London: Kegan Paul, 1925), p. 33.

38. André Siegfried, *America Comes of Age* (New York: Harcourt, Brace & Co., 1928), p. 349. A year after its first publication this book had gone through eight printings.

39. R. M. Fox, *The Triumphant Machine* (London: Hogarth, 1928), pp. 123–24.

40. S. D. Schmalhausen, ed. *Behold America!* (New York: Farrar & Rinehart, 1931), p. 724.

41. Henry Ford, *My Life and Work* (Garden City, N.Y.: Garden City Publishing Co., 1922), p. 104.

42. Ibid., pp. 86, 103, 105.

43. Henry Ford, *My Philosophy of Industry* (New York: Coward-McCann, 1929), p. 18.

44. Ibid., pp. 11–12, 17–18.

45. Henry Ford, *Moving Forward* (Garden City, N.Y.: Doubleday, Doran and Co., 1930), pp. 146–47, 249–50.

46. Henry Ford, *365 of Henry Ford's Sayings*, ed. P. M. Martin (New York: League-For-A-Living, 1923), pp. 44–45.

47. Quotes in Gamaliel Bradford, *The Quick and the Dead* (Boston: Houghton-Mifflin, 1931), p. 133.

48. Ibid., pp. 146, 118.

49. Frederick Winslow Taylor, *The Principles of Scientific Management* (New York: Norton, 1967), p. 59.

50. Ibid., pp. 40, 74, 94.

51. See Samuel Haber, *Efficiency and Uplift: Scientific Management in the Progressive Era, 1890–1920* (Chicago: University of Chicago Press, 1964), pp. 43, 48, 63.

52. According to Ford, *My Life,* p. 106, "the work in each department is classified according to its desirability and skill into Classes 'A', 'B', and 'C', each class having anywhere from ten to thirty different operations." These classes are evocative of the Galtonian classificatory system which, reversed and using Greek letters, forms the basis of Huxley's. Huxley refers specifically to Galton's categories as early as *Those Barren Leaves* (1925), p. 292. See also Francis Galton, *Hereditary Genius* (London: Macmillan, 1914), p. 327. (This work was first published in 1869.) In this connection it is interesting to note that in the last year of his life Galton composed a fragmentary eugenic utopia, "Kantsaywhere," in which a Eugenic College would own the country and direct a Council that would then improve the animal and human population. According to C. P. Blacker, *Eugenics, Galton and After* (London: Gerald Duckworth, 1952), p. 122, Galton seems to have been possessed by the idea that "power should finally lie with a eugenic *corps d'élite* or caste" and that "reproductive functions were to be regulated by an oligarchy selected by tests."

53. Ford, *Moving Foreward*, pp. 247–48.

54. Stuart Chase, *Men and Machines* (New York: Macmillan, 1931), pp. 35, 120, 254, 346.

55. Ralph Bosodi, *This Ugly Civilization* (New York: Simon & Schuster, 1929), pp. 65, 71–72.

56. Ibid., pp. 111, 314, 357.

57. Georges Duhamel, *America the Menace, Scenes from the Life of the Future*, trans. C. M. Thompson (London: Allen & Unwin, 1931), pp. 32, 48, 64, 194, 196–97. See also Lucien Romier, *Qui sera le maître, Europe ou Amérique?* (Paris: Hachette, 1924).

58. Ibid., p. 210.

59. Huxley had in fact foreseen a future society purely dependent on machines in

"Boundaries of Utopia," *Virginia Quarterly Review* 7 (January 1931): 49.

The anti-machine future is, of course, most memorably depicted in Samuel Butler's *Erewhon* (1872), for a reedition of which Huxley once wrote a preface. In *Erewhon* the hostility to machines derives ultimately from the fear that machines will one day supplant man, a fear not shared by the new world state. There is, however, a shared hostility to scientific research, as well as other resemblances: Butler's "straighteners" or soul-doctors anticipate Huxley's psychological conditioning; children are sent to "Deformatories" if they are deficient in "immoral sense"; external beauty is much prized and death belittled; conformity—or worship of the goddess Ydgrun (Mrs. Grundy)—is the primary law and individuality is frowned upon: ". . . genius was like offences—needs must that it come, but woe unto that man through whom it comes. A man's business, they hold, is to think as his neighbours do, for heaven help him if he thinks good what they count bad." The past is also despised as bunk: there is a Society for the Suppression of Useless Knowledge and for the Completer Obliteration of the Past. See Samuel Butler, *Erewhon, Or Over the Range* (London: Jonathan Cape, 1927), pp. 221–22.

Chapter 5. Conclusion: The Two Futures: A.F. 632 and 1984

1. A. E. Dyson, *The Crazy Fabric, Essays in Irony* (London: Macmillan, 1965), p. 175.

2. George Kateb, *Utopia and Its Enemies* (Glencoe, Ill.: The Free Press, 1963), p. 126.

3. In a letter to his son Matthew, dated October 23, 1949, Huxley announces the completion of his "essay book," referring almost certainly to *Themes and Variations*. This announcement, made two days after the letter to Orwell, suggests that Huxley must have incorporated his remarks on Orwell into the almost completed typescript of the book. As a curious item of literary history it is perhaps also worth noting that Orwell (then called Eric Blair) had been Huxley's pupil at Eton while the latter was teaching there between 1917 and 1919. Orwell was, a fellow student remembered, chiefly impressed by Huxley's virtuosic use of language. See Jeffrey Meyers, *A Reader's Guide to George Orwell* (London: Thames & Hudson, 1975), p. 31.

4. Already in the 1946 foreword, however, Huxley had revised his original forecast to allow for the possibility that "the horror may be upon us in a single century" (xv).

5. Zamiatin, a disillusioned Bolshevik, wrote *We* in 1920–21, but was not allowed to publish it in the Soviet Union. The original Russian version was first printed in New York in 1952. See C. Moody, "Zamiatin's *We* and English Antiutopian Fiction," *UNISA English Studies* 14 (1976): 24.

6. George Orwell, *The Collected Essays, Journalism, and Letters*, ed. Sonia Orwell and Ian Angus (London: Secker & Warburg, 1968), 3:95.

7. Orwell, *Collected Essays*, 4:72.

8. Ibid., p. 485.

9. Quoted in Moody, "Zamiatin," p. 29. Some of the resemblances between *We* and *Brave New World* may have arisen from the fact that they share a common (satiric) debt to H. G. Wells. As Huxley admitted, *Brave New World* started out as a parody of Wells's *Men Like Gods* (1923), and Zamiatin, who was steeped in Wells and had written two essays on his work, met Wells for the first time while the latter was working on *Men Like Gods*. For Zamiatin's contacts with Wells, see Moody, "Zamiatin," p. 30.

10. Orwell's glibness in this respect rubbed off on his friend George Woodcock, who, in *The Crystal Spirit, A Study of George Orwell* (Boston: Little, Brown, & Co., 1966), p. 209, flatly asserts that "the book that influenced Orwell most was Zamiatin's *We*, from which Huxley had already borrowed copiously in writing *Brave New World*." By the time Wood-

cock got around to publishing his book on Huxley, however, he had changed his mind a little. On the one hand, he still found it unlikely that Huxley had not read *We* before writing *Brave New World,* but on the other he was prepared to admit that "its influence on *Brave New World* is obviously—if it exists—less profound and direct [than *We's* influence on *Nineteen Eighty-Four*], despite the many striking resemblances between the two novels." See *Dawn and the Darkest Hour: A Study of Aldous Huxley* (New York: Viking, 1972), p. 174. More recently, James Connors has attempted to minimize the influence of Zamiatin even on *Nineteen Eighty-Four,* maintaining that the basic debt is only to the Benefactor, the Big Brother figure in *We.* For the rest, Connors believes that the differences far outweigh the similarities. See "Zamiatin's *We* and the Genesis of *1984*," *MFS,* 21 (Spring 1975): 116. Whatever the merits of this argument (considerable, I would say), it is clear from the letter to Struve, if nothing else, that Orwell was planning something like *Nineteen Eighty-Four* before he had read *We.*

11. George Orwell, *Keep the Aspidistra Flying* (London: Secker & Warburg, 1962), p. 110. A year later, in *The Road to Wigan Pier* (London: Heinemann, 1965), p. 202, Orwell had noted that *Brave New World* "probably expresses what a majority of thinking people feel about machine-civilisation." Critics in general have tended to focus on the manifest and admitted differences between *Brave New World* and *Nineteen Eighty-Four* rather than on the equally manifest but less-admitted similarities. See, for example, J. H. Westlake, "Aldous Huxley's *Brave New World* and George Orwell's *Nineteen Eighty-Four:* A Comparative Study," *Die Neueren Sprachen* 71, n.s. 21 (1972): 96.

12. George Orwell, *Nineteen Eighty-Four* (London: Secker & Warburg, 1965), p. 8. All further references will be included in the text, by page number enclosed in parentheses.

13. In one of the chapters of Goldstein's "Book" Orwell seems to allude critically to *Brave New World.* "It was possible," Goldstein/Trotsky writes, "no doubt to imagine a society in which *wealth,* in the sense of personal possessions and luxuries, should be evenly distributed, while *power* remained in the hands of a small privileged caste. But in practice such a society could not long remain stable." Why not? Because the less privileged castes would in time become educated, start thinking for themselves and then summarily remove the privileged caste. "In the long run, a hierarchical society was only possible on the basis of poverty and ignorance" (195). Orwell had earlier leveled precisely the same charge against *Brave New World* in a 1940 review of a reprint of Jack London's *The Iron Heel.* "Though *Brave New World* was a brilliant caricature of the present (the present of 1930)," Orwell writes, "it probably casts no light on the future. No society of that kind would last more than a couple of generations, because a ruling class which thought principally in terms of a 'good time' would soon lose its vitality. A ruling class has got to have a strict morality, a quasi-religious belief in itself, a mystique." See Orwell, *Collected Essays,* 2:31. This argument is also made by Theodor W. Adorno who, in his 1942 essay on *Brave New World,* attacks Huxley for having based his future state on a theory of sexual license. All dictatorships, Adorno maintains, are puritan and anti-sexual. See his *Prismen* (Berlin: Suhrkamp, [1955]), p. 124.

Works Cited

Adorno, Theodor W. "Aldous Huxley und die Utopie," in *Prismen*. Berlin: Suhrkamp, [1955].

Becker, Carl L. *The Heavenly City of the Eighteenth-Century Philosophers*. New Haven, Conn.: Yale University Press, 1959.

Beloff, John. "The Mind-Body Problem As It Now Stands," *Virginia Quarterly Review* 49 (Spring 1973), 251–64.

Benedict, Ruth. *Patterns of Culture*. London: Routledge & Sons, 1935.

Berdyaev, Nicholas. *The End of Our Time*. London: Sheed & Ward, 1933.

Bernal, J. D. *The Social Function of Science*. Cambridge, Mass.: MIT Press, 1967.

————. *The World, the Flesh and the Devil: An Enquiry into the Future of the Three Enemies of the Rational Soul*. Bloomington, Ind.: Indiana University Press, 1969.

Blacker, C. P. *Eugenics: Galton and After*. London: Duckworth, 1952.

Borsodi, Ralph. *This Ugly Civilization*. New York: Simon & Schuster, 1929.

Bradford, Gamaliel. *The Quick and the Dead*. Boston: Houghton & Mifflin, 1931.

Bunzel, Ruth L. *Zuñi Texts*. Publications of the American Ethnological Society, Vol. 15. New York: Stechert, 1933.

Butler, Samuel. *Erewhon, Or Over the Range*. London: Jonathan Cape, 1927.

Calverton, V. F. and S. D. Schmalhausen, eds. *Sex in Civilization*. New York: Macmillan, 1929.

Chase, Stuart. *Men and Machines*. New York: Macmillan, 1931.

Clark, Ronald. *JBS*. London: Hodder & Stoughton, 1968.

Colletti, Lucio. *From Rousseau to Lenin: Studies in Ideology and Society*. London: NLB, 1972.

Conklin, E. M. *Heredity and Environment*. Princeton, N.J.: Princeton University Press, 1922.

Connors, James. "Zamiatin's *We* and the Genesis of *1984*," *Modern Fiction Studies* 21 (Spring 1975): 107–24.

Crocker, L. G. *Rousseau's Social Contract: An Interpretive Essay*. Cleveland: Western Reserve, 1968.

Cushing, Frank Hamilton. *My Adventures in Zuni*. Santa Fe, N.M.: The Peripatetic Press, 1941.

———. "Outlines of Zuni Creation Myths," *Annual Report of the Bureau of Ethnology* 13 (1891–92): 325–447.

Diderot, Denis. *Rêve d'Alembert*, ed. Paul Vernière. Paris: Marcel Didier, 1951.

Dostoevski, Fyodor. *The Brothers Karamazov*, trans. Constance Garnett. New York: New American Library, 1957.

———. *The Possessed*, trans. Constance Garnett. New York: Modern Library, 1936.

Duhamel, Georges. *America the Menace, Scenes from the Life of the Future*, trans. C. M. Thompson. London: Allen & Unwin, 1931.

Dumas, Georges. *Psychologie de deux messies positivistes*. Paris: Félix Alcan, 1905.

Dyson, A. E. *The Crazy Fabric: Essays in Irony*. London: Macmillan, 1965.

Fay, Elliott. *Lorenzo in Search of the Sun*. London: Vision Press, 1955.

Flaubert, Gustave. *La Tentation de Saint Antoine*. Paris: Louis Conard, 1924.

Ford, Henry. *Moving Forward*. Garden City, N.Y.: Doubleday, Doran & Co., 1930.

———. *My Life and Work*. Garden City, N.Y.: Garden City Publishing Co., 1922.

———. *My Philosophy of Industry*. New York: Coward-McCann, 1929.

———. *365 of Henry Ford's Sayings*, ed. P. M. Martin. New York: League-For-A-Living, 1923.

Fourier, Charles. *Design for Utopia*, ed. Charles Gide. New York: Schocken Books, 1971.

Fox, R. M. *The Triumphant Machine*. London: Hogarth, 1928.

Freud, Sigmund. *A General Selection from the Works*, ed. John Rickman. Garden City, N.Y.: Doubleday, 1957.

————. *Works*, trans. James Strachey. London: Hogarth, 1961.

Fuelop-Miller, René. *The Mind and Face of Bolshevism*. New York: Harper & Row, 1965.

Fuller, Colonel J. F. C. *Atlantis, Or America and the Future*. London: Kegan Paul, [1926].

Galton, Francis. *Hereditary Genius*. London: Macmillan, 1914.

Garrett, Garet. *Ouroboros, Or the Mechanical Extension of Mankind*. London: Kegan Paul, 1925.

Gibbs, Philip. *The Day After To-morrow*. London: Hutchinson, [1927].

Goddard, Pliny Earle. *Indians of the Southwest*. New York: American Museum of Natural History, 1913.

Goldring, Douglas. *Odd Man Out*. London: Chapman & Hall, 1935.

Haber, Samuel. *Efficiency and Uplift: Scientific Management in the Progressive Era, 1890–1920*. Chicago: University of Chicago Press, 1964.

Haeberlin, H. K. "The Idea of Fertilization in the Culture of the Pueblo Indians," *Memoirs of the American Anthropological Association* 3 (1916): 1–55.

Haldane, Charlotte. "Dr. Huxley and Mr. Arnold [Review of *Brave New World*]," *Nature* 129 (23 April 1932): 598.

Haldane, J. B. S. "Biological Possibilities for the Human Species in the Next Ten Thousand Years," in *Man and His Future*, ed. Gordon Wolstenholme. London: J. & A. Churchill, 1963.

————. *Daedalus*. New York: Dutton, 1924.

————. *Science and Human Life*. New York: Harper, 1933.

Haldane, J. S. *Mechanism, Life and Personality*. London: John Murray, 1913.

Heard, Gerald. "The Poignant Prophet," *The Kenyon Review* 27 (Winter 1965): 49–70.

Hicks, Granville. "Review of *Brave New World*," *The New Republic* 69 (10 February 1932): 354.

Hillegas, Mark. *The Future as Nightmare: H. G. Wells and the Anti-Utopians*. New York: Oxford, 1967.

Hogben, Lancelot. *The Nature of Living Matter*. New York: Knopf, 1931.

Huxley, Aldous. "Aldous Huxley" [interview]," *The Little Review* 12 (May 1929): 48–49.

————. *Antic Hay*. London: Chatto & Windus, 1923.

————. "Boundaries of Utopia," *Virginia Quarterly Review* 7 (January 1931): 47–54.

————. *Brave New World*. London: Chatto & Windus, 1932.

————. "Brave New World," *Life* 25 (20 September 1948), 63–64, 66–68, 70.

————. *Brave New World Revisited*. London: Chatto & Windus, 1959.

————. *Brief Candles*. London: Chatto & Windus, 1930.

————. "The Cold-Blooded Romantics," *Vanity Fair* 30 (March 1928): 64, 104.

————. *Crome Yellow*. London: Chatto & Windus, 1921.

————. *Do What You Will*. London: Chatto & Windus, 1929.

————. *The Human Situation*. New York: Harper & Row, 1977.

————. "If My Library Burned Tonight," *Home and Garden* 92 (November 1947): 185.

————. *Letters*, ed. Grover Smith. London: Chatto & Windus, 1969.

————. *Music at Night*. London: Chatto & Windus, 1931.

————. "Obstacle Race," *The Adelphi* (April 1931), 34–42.

————. *On the Margin*. London: Chatto & Windus, 1956.

————. "The Outlook for American Culture: Some Reflections in a Machine Age," *Harper's Magazine* 155 (August 1927): 265–70.

————. "Preface" to Knud Merrild, *A Poet and Two Painters*. London: George Routledge, 1938.

————. *Themes and Variations*. London: Chatto & Windus, 1950.

————. *Those Barren Leaves*. London: Chatto & Windus, 1950.

————. "A Treatise on Drugs," *Chicago Herald & Examiner* (10 October 1931), 11.

————. "Whither Are We Civilising?" *Vanity Fair* 30 (April 1928): 64, 124.

Huxley, Julian, ed. *Aldous Huxley, 1894–1963*. London: Chatto & Windus, 1965.

Huxley, Julian. *Memories*. New York: Harper & Row, 1970.

Jennings, H. S. *Prometheus, Or Biology and the Advancement of Man*. London: Kegan Paul, [1926].

Kateb, George. *Utopia and Its Enemies*. Glencoe, Ill.: The Free Press, 1963.

Krutch, J. W. "Modern Love and Modern Fiction," in *The Modern Temper*. New York: Harcourt, Brace & Co., 1929.

Laski, Harold J. *Faith, Reason and Civilisation*. London: Gollancz, 1944.

Lawrence, D. H. *Letters*, ed. H. T. Moore. Geneva: Heron Books, [1962].

————. *Mornings in Mexico*. London: Martin Secker, 1927.

————. *Phoenix*, ed. E. D. McDonald. London: Heinemann, 1936.

————. *Phoenix II*, ed. Warren Roberts and H. T. Moore. New York: Penguin, 1978.

————. *Poems*. Geneva: Heron, 1964.

————. *Selected Literary Criticism*, ed. Anthony Beal. London: Macmillan, 1953.

Leach, Gerald. *The Biocrats*. London: Jonathan Cape, 1970.

LeBon, Gustave. *The Crowd*. London: Fisher Unwin, 1896.

Leuba, J. H. *The Psychology of Religious Mysticism*. New York: Harcourt, Brace & Co., 1925.

Ludovici, A. M. *Lysistrata, Or Woman's Future and Future Woman*. London: Kegan Paul, [1926].

Lytton, Edward Bulwer. *The Coming Race*. London: Oxford, 1928.

Malinowski, Bronislaw. *Sex and Repression in Savage Society*. New York: Harcourt, Brace & Co., 1927.

Mann, Klaus. *Der Wendepunkt, Ein Lebensbericht*. Frankfurt a. M.: Fischer Verlag, 1952.

Manuel, F. E. and F. P. eds. *French Utopias*. New York: The Free Press, 1966.

Manuel, F. E. *The New World of Saint-Simon*. Cambridge: Harvard University Press, 1956.

Manuel, F. E. and F. P. *Utopian Thought in the Western World*. Cambridge: Harvard University Press, 1979.

Mead, Margaret. *Coming of Age in Samoa*. New York: Blue Ribbon Books, 1932.

Meckier, Jerome. "A Neglected Huxley 'Preface': His Earliest Synopsis of *Brave New World*," *Twentieth Century Literature* 25 (Spring 1979): 1–20.

————. "Our Ford, Our Freud and the Behaviourist Conspiracy in Huxley's *Brave New World*," *Thalia* 1 (1977–78): 35–59.

————. "Shakespeare and Aldous Huxley," *Shakespeare Quarterly* 22 (Spring 1971): 129–35.

Meyers, Jeffrey. *A Reader's Guide to George Orwell*. London: Thames & Hudson, 1975.

Moody, C. "Zamiatin's *We* and English Antiutopian Fiction," *UNISA English Studies* 14 (1976): 24–33.

Muller, H. J. *Out of the Night, A Biologist's View of the Future*. London: Gollancz, 1936.

Mumford, Lewis. *The Pentagon of Power*. New York: Harcourt, Brace, Jovanovich, 1970.

————. *The Story of Utopias*. New York: Boni & Liveright, 1922.

Myers, F. W. H. *Human Personality and Its Survival of Bodily Death*. New York: Longmans, 1904.

Needham, Joseph. "Biology and Mr. Huxley [Review of *Brave New World*]," *Scrutiny* 1 (May 1932): 76–79.

————. *Man a Machine*. London: Kegan Paul, 1927.

Newman, Stanley. *Zuni Dictionary*. Bloomington, Ind.: Indiana Research Center in Anthropology, Folklore and Linguistics, 1958.

Orwell, George. *Collected Essays, Journalism, and Letters*, ed. Sonia Orwell and Ian Angus. London: Secker & Warburg, 1968.

————. *Keep the Aspidistra Flying*. London: Secker & Warburg, 1962.

————. *Nineteen Eighty-Four*. London: Secker & Warburg, 1965.

————. *The Road to Wigan Pier*. London: Heinemann, 1965.

Parrinder, Patrick, ed. *H. G. Wells: The Critical Heritage*. London: Routledge & Kegal Paul, 1972.

Parsons, Elsie Clewes. *Pueblo Indian Religion*. Chicago: University of Chicago Press, 1939.

Patmore, Derek. *Private History*. London: Jonathan Cape, 1960.

Petre, M. D. "Bolshevist Ideals and the 'Brave New World,'" *The Hibbert Journal* 31 (October 1932–July 1933): 61–71.

Powell, J. A. A. "The Vanishing Values—Huxley's Permutations of *The Tempest*," Ph.D. dissertation, University of Utah, 1973.

Riasanovsky, N. V. *The Teaching of Charles Fourier*. Berkeley and Los Angeles: University of California Press, 1969.

Romanof, Panteleimon. *Without Cherry Blossom*, trans. L. Zarine. New York: Scribners, 1932.

Romier, Lucien. *Qui sera le maître, Europe ou Amérique?* Paris: Hachette, 1924.

Roppen, Georg. *Evolution and Poetic Belief*. Oslo: Oslo University Press, 1956.

Rostrand, Jean. *Science et Génération*. Paris: Fasquelle, 1948.

Rousseau, Jean-Jacques. "Discours sur l'origine de l'inégalité parmi les hommes," in *Du Contrat social au principes du droit politique*. Paris: Garnier, 1962.

Routh, H. V. *English Literature and Ideas in the Twentieth Century*. London: Methuen, 1946.

Russell, Bertrand. *The Conquest of Happiness*. New York: The Book League of America, 1930.

————. *Icarus*. London: Kegan Paul, 1924.

————. *Marriage and Morals*. London: Allen & Unwin, 1929.

————. *The Scientific Outlook*. Glencoe, Ill.: The Free Press, 1931.

Russell, Dora. *The Right to Be Happy*. London: Routledge & Sons, 1927.

Schmalhausen, S. D., ed. *Behold America!* New York: Farrar & Rinehart, 1931.

Schmalhausen, S. D. *Why We Misbehave*. Garden City, N.Y.: Garden City Publishing Co., 1928.

Shaw, G. B. S. *Complete Plays*. London: Constable, 1931.

Shklar, Judith N. *After Utopia*. Princeton, N.J.: Princeton University Press, 1957.

————. *Men and Citizens: A Study of Rousseau's Social Theory*. Cambridge: Cambridge University Press, 1969.

Siegfried, André. *America Comes of Age*. New York: Harcourt, Brace & Co., 1928.

Smith, Grover. *T. S. Eliot's Poetry and Plays: A Study in Sources and Meaning*. Chicago: University of Chicago Press, 1956.

Snow, Melinda. "The Gray Parody in *Brave New World*," *Papers on Language and Literature* 13 (Winter 1977): 85–88.

Spengler, Oswald. *The Decline of the West*, trans. C. F. Atkinson. New York: Knopf, 1950.

Sullivan, J. W. N. *Gallio, Or the Tyranny of Science*. London: Kegan Paul, [1927].

————. *The Limitations of Science*. London: Chatto & Windus, 1933.

Talmon, J. L. *Origins of Totalitarian Democracy*. London: Secker & Warburg, 1952.

Taylor, Frederick Winslow. *The Principles of Scientific Management*. New York: Norton, 1967.

Taylor, G. R. *The Biological Time-Bomb*. London: Panther Books, 1972.

Thody, Philip. *Aldous Huxley*. London: Studio Vista, 1973.

Tocqueville, Alexis de. *Democracy in America*, trans. Henry Reeve. New York: Colonial Press, 1899.

Uexkuell, J. J. von. *Theoretical Biology*. London: Kegan Paul, 1926.

Wagar, W. Warren. *H. G. Wells and the World State*. New Haven, Conn.: Yale University Press, 1961.

Warburg, Fredric. *An Occupation for Gentlemen*. London: Hutchinson, 1959.

Ward A. C. *The Nineteen-Twenties*. London: Methuen, 1930.

Ward, Henslow. *Builders of Decision*. Indianapolis, Ind.: Bobbs-Merrill, 1931.

Watson, J. B. and William McDougall, *The Battle of Behaviorism*. London: Kegan Paul, 1928.

Watson, John B. *Behaviorism*. 2d ed. London: Kegan Paul, 1931.

Watt, Donald ed. *Aldous Huxley: The Critical Heritage*. London: Routledge & Kegan Paul, 1975.

Watt, Donald. "The Manuscript Revisions of *Brave New World*," *Journal of English and Germanic Philology* 77 (July 1978): 367–82.

Wells, H. G. *The First Men in the Moon*. London: George Newnes, 1901.

———. *Men Like Gods*. New York: Macmillan, 1923.

———. *The New World Order*. New York: Knopf, 1940.

———. *Seven Famous Novels*. Garden City, N.Y.: Garden City Publishing Co., 1934.

———. *Tales of Space and Time*. Leipzig: Tauchnitz, 1900.

———. *When the Sleeper Wakes*. New York: Harper's 1899.

Westlake, J. H. "Aldous Huxley's *Brave New World* and George Orwell's *Nineteen Eighty-Four:* A Comparative Study," *Die Neueren Sprachen* 71 (1972): 94–102.

Wickes, George and Ray Frazer, "Aldous Huxley," *Writers at Work: The 'Paris Review' Interviews*, Second Series. London: Secker & Warburg, 1963.

Wilson, R. H. "*Brave New World* as Shakespeare Criticism," *The Shakespeare Association Bulletin* 21 (July 1946): 99–107.

Woodcock, George. *The Crystal Spirit: A Study of George Orwell*. Boston: Little, Brown & Co., 1966.

———. *Dawn and the Darkest Hour: A Study of Aldous Huxley*. New York: Viking, 1972.

Woodger, J. H. *Biological Principles*. New York: Harcourt, Brace & Co., 1929.

Index